PRAY
SUNDA

C000192578

Richard Atherton

a redemptorist publication

(Year C)

Published by Redemptorist Publications
Alphonsus House Chawton Hants GU34 3HQ
www.shineonline.net

First printed October 2003

Design Orchid Design

ISBN 0 85231 281 4

Printed in Britain by
J.W. Arrowsmith Limited Bristol BS3 2NT

Redemptorist
PUBLICATIONS

Contents

Foreword

In his letter to the Christian community in Rome, Paul lists some of the many blessings that God bestowed upon Israel – adoption as "son of God", the glory of God's presence in the desert and in Jerusalem, the covenants, the Law, the Temple worship, the promises, the patriarchs and, the glorious climax, Jesus Christ himself (Romans 9:4-5). Of course the list is not exhaustive. If it were, it would surely have included an explicit mention of the psalms, those divinely inspired hymns which, in the words of a recent Vatican document, 'constitute the very heart of the Old Testament'[1]. Nor have they lost any of their value with the coming of Christ: in the New Testament the Psalter is quoted more often than any other book of the Old Testament with the possible exception of Isaiah. In fact, the psalms have gained a new level of significance in the light of the mystery of Christ. And so, from earliest times, Christian people have embraced them as an ideal form of prayer, a sharing in the very prayers once used by our Lord. "From the beginning of the Church" wrote Pius X "the divinely inspired psalms in the Bible have had a remarkable influence in deepening the devotion of the faithful..."[2]

Though praying the psalms has been a marked feature of Christian worship down the ages, it seems to have suffered a decline, in the Catholic community at any rate, for several centuries. The psalms still formed the backbone of the divine office but since the Office was in Latin and was generally regarded as the special preserve of the priest, they scarcely affected the majority of the faithful. And in the Mass itself the only use of the psalms was limited to the recitation of a couple of verses from a psalm (again in Latin) just before the gospel. It was the Second Vatican Council (1962-65) that restored them to their rightful place in the liturgy of the Church. The divine office, now in the vernacular and called, significantly, the Prayer of the Church (the whole Church), has become increasingly accessible to lay people, many of whom have made sections of the Office, or even the whole Office, a regular part of their prayer. Even more importantly perhaps, there is a much more generous use of the psalms in the Mass through the introduction of the responsorial psalm. Week by week the psalms are now heard in our churches and their words have become familiar sounds in our ears – and, in many cases, in our hearts.

However, greater familiarity with the psalms has also revealed the need for help if the full value of these ancient prayers and their significance for men and women of the third millennium are to be appreciated. As the Council explains, it is necessary to 'attune our minds', our understanding, to the psalms[3]. The first two volumes[4] in this series represent an attempt to provide such help for those who, Sunday by Sunday, seek to pray (not merely recite) the responsorial psalm, just as the author's earlier books tried to do the same for those who pray the psalms that make up the Prayer of the Church[5]. The pattern of this book is similar to that followed in the books for Years A and B. There are three sections for each Sunday. The first is a brief explanation of all three of the Sunday's readings and an indication of how the responsorial psalm fits into the overall theme. The second, taking its inspiration from Mary who 'pondered things over in her heart', is called Prayerful Ponderings and is an explanation of the psalm in some detail, an opening up of its meaning. The third, entitled Let us Pray, is an attempt to sum up in prayer what has been pondered in the previous section.

It is my hope that this book will be useful not only to those who wish to use the Sunday psalm for personal prayer but also for those who, in their ministry as Readers, have the privilege of leading worshippers in praying the responsorial psalm at Mass. One of the surest ways of bringing the responsorial psalm to life for the congregation is though the example of readers (or singers) who have themselves taken the trouble to make the psalm their own.

I wish to express my indebtedness to the many scholars whose writings have helped me in preparing this book, to my brother Bernard whose art work once again embellishes this volume and to the staff of Redemptorist Publications for their help and encouragement.

Notes

1 *The Jewish People and their Sacred Scriptures in the Christian Bible §47-* Pontifical Bible Commission 2001

2 *Apostolic Constitution on the Psalter in the Divine Office*

3 *The Constitution on the Sacred Liturgy §90*

4 *Praying the Sunday Psalms (Year A)* and *Praying the Sunday Psalms (Year B)*

5 *New Light: Discovering the Psalms in the Prayer of the Church* – Redemptorist Publications (1993) and *Praying the Prayer of the Church* – Redemptorist Publications (1998)

ADVENT

A shoot shall spring from the stock of Jesse

ADVENT

'As once through Mary's flesh you came,
To save us from our sin and shame,
So now, Redeemer, by your grace,
Come heal again our fallen race.

'And when on that last judgment day,
We rise to glory from decay,
Then come again, O Saviour blest,
And bring us to eternal rest.'
(Irvin Udulutsch OSB)

First Sunday of Advent

Today's readings capture the notion of Advent waiting: the waiting for Christ's coming in the past, the waiting for his coming in the present (especially in the liturgy) and the waiting for that day in the future when he will come again.

Though it looked as though the promise of a Davidic dynasty was not going to be fulfilled, the sixth century prophet Jeremiah (33:14-16) gives the assurance that in fact it will be and that already a Branch is growing in the house of David.

If Jeremiah's words look forward to the birth of the Messiah (the first coming), today's gospel (Luke 21:25-28, 34-36) looks forward to a future time when Christ will come again to judge (his second coming); hence the emphasis on being ready for his arrival. (The larger-than-life picture of cosmic upheaval is typical of this type of writing in the Old Testament and in the New.)

In the second reading (1 Thessalonians 3:12–4:2) Paul focuses on the present: he exhorts the people of Thessalonica, in words equally applicable to us today, to live lives worthy of their calling and in particular to grow in love of each other and of the whole human race, as they await the Lord's return.

Meanwhile the responsorial psalm, taken from Psalm 24, begs for God's help and praises his faithfulness and love. Though there is no explicit reference to waiting upon God, that idea seems to be implied.

Prayerful Ponderings

'To you, O Lord, I lift up my soul.'

These, the opening words of Psalm 24, are rich in significance. In Israel it was customary to pray with arms uplifted, stretched out towards the heavens. To say 'to you, O Lord, I lift up my soul' was putting into words what that action meant: to you, Lord, I raise up my whole self, my innermost self, in complete trust and confidence. How fitting that these words should be the refrain of this Sunday's responsorial psalm. Each time we repeat them we are expressing our trust, we are acknowledging, in a truly Advent spirit, that we wait upon the Lord: wait for his coming at Christmas, wait for his coming at the end of time, wait for his coming now at this Eucharist, as well as in the events of this day – and every day.

'Lord, make me know your ways. Lord, teach me your paths. Make me walk in your truth and teach me: for you are God my Saviour.'

The psalmist expresses a longing which we share, the longing to be taught 'your ways' and 'your paths'. Taking God seriously means that we do not wish to be left to our own devices; we want him to be our teacher, we want him to make known to us the way we should go, for after all he is our 'God', our 'Saviour'. The sense of looking to God for instruction is one of the striking features of the whole of this psalm.

'The Lord is good and upright. He shows the path to those who stray, he guides the humble in the right path; he teaches his way to the poor.'

If there were any question about why we should seek God's instruction, here is the answer: because he is 'good and upright'. He 'is good' and that ensures that our own best interests are always served; he 'is upright' and that means that there is no deviousness in him, he is straightforward in all his dealings with us. A modern writer has said that 'being a creature is in danger of becoming a lost art'. It's so easy to forget that we are small, finite creatures. The remedy is to be 'humble' and 'poor', deeply aware of our limitations, for then, the psalmist assures us, we shall receive the guidance and the teaching of the Lord.

'His ways are faithfulness and love for those who keep his covenant and will.'

The psalm offers a further reason for seeking the guidance of the Lord. It is that those who acknowledge, by the way they live their lives, God's 'covenant' friendship with them, discover that all 'his ways' are characterised by 'faithfulness and love'.

'The Lord's friendship is for those who revere him; to them he reveals his covenant.'

The fact is that those who hold him in reverence experience his 'friendship' and day by day they discover – because 'he reveals' it to them – the rich meaning of 'his covenant'

LET US PRAY: *Heavenly Father, be with us in our Advent waiting; teach us the paths we are to follow if we are to be ready for the celebration of your Son's birth at Christmastide and for that day when he will come again at the end of time.*

Second Sunday of Advent

The splendid poem of the first reading (Baruch 5:1-9), attributed to Baruch the secretary of the prophet Jeremiah, tells of the restoration of Jerusalem after the dark days of exile.

The gospel (Luke 3:1-6) speaks of a still more glorious restoration: John the Baptist, herald of the Lord, appears, announcing that all humankind are to see 'the salvation of God'.

St Paul, in the second reading (Philippians 1:3-6, 8-11), urges his friends to live in such a way that they may enjoy the fullness of reconciliation with God when Jesus comes again in his glory.

Psalm 125, today's responsorial psalm, begs that God, who in times past brought deliverance to his people, will act again on their behalf.

Prayerful Ponderings

'When the Lord delivered Zion from bondage, it seemed like a dream.'

Psalm 125 is the seventh of the fifteen 'Songs of Ascent'. We can imagine the pilgrims on their way up to Jerusalem singing this song, not only to remind themselves of God's favours in the past but also to remind God as well, in the hope of encouraging him to do the same again in present difficulties. There is no way of knowing exactly what 'Zion' (here standing for the whole people) was 'delivered' from, though it may well have been the exile. In any event it clearly surpassed all expectations, so much so that the psalmist can only say that 'it seemed like a dream'.

'Then was our mouth filled with laughter, on our lips there were songs.'

The incredible event brought about an unbelievable transformation: faces that had been heavy with sadness and sorrow were suddenly transformed with joyful 'laughter' and lips that had uttered groans now sang joyous 'songs'. Whatever may have been the surprise event which sparked off such happy consequences, one thing is certain: it pales in significance when compared with the event that we are soon to celebrate – the coming of Christ and the deliverance he will bring. That is why our Advent waiting is always shot through with joy: we delight in the mighty deeds of our God.

'The heathens themselves said: "What marvels the Lord worked for them!" What marvels the Lord worked for us! Indeed we were glad.'

The psalmist recalls how even 'the heathens' were taken aback by the 'marvels the Lord worked' for his people. And as for the people themselves, they could only share the amazement of their pagan neighbours and confess that the Lord had in all truth done wonders for them and 'indeed we were glad'.

'Deliver us, O Lord, from our bondage as streams in dry land.'

The memory of what the Lord had done gives them courage to plead with him to 'deliver' them from current 'bondage' and restore their happiness. Thinking of the way a desert region is quickly transformed when the rains begin to fall upon its parched water courses, they pray that they may experience a similar change of fortune.

'Those who are sowing in tears will sing when they reap. They go out, they go out, full of tears, carrying seed for the sowing: they come back, they come back, full of song, carrying their sheaves.'

Similarly, thinking of the contrast between the 'tears' of the farmers as they set about 'sowing' their seed and the songs they sing when it comes to harvest time, they pray that their tears may give way to joy. In the spirit of today's readings, we too pray that whatever the hardships and 'tears' of our present life, we may one day come safely home 'carrying [our] sheaves', that 'perfect goodness which', Paul tells us, 'Christ produces in us for the glory and praise of God'.

LET US PRAY: *As we joyfully await the birth of Christ, when 'all mankind shall see the salvation of our God', we also plead, mighty Lord, that our lives may be a preparation for the Day when Christ will come again and our tears are turned into everlasting joy.*

Third Sunday of Advent

Today's readings catch notes both of joy and of fear as they speak of God's coming to his people. The seventh-century prophet Zephaniah (3:14-18), addressing those who are lowly and recognise their absolute need of God, assures them that 'the Lord... is in your midst', dancing 'with shouts of joy for you'.

In the gospel (Luke 3:10-18) John the Baptist advises the people how they are to live their daily lives and warns that the coming of the Messiah will separate wheat from chaff; it will be good news for the former but not for the latter.

Paul in the second reading (Philippians 4:4-7) urges his friends at Philippi 'to be happy... in the Lord', to put aside all worries and to trust in God.

On this occasion the responsorial psalm is taken not from the Psalter but from the book of Isaiah. Like other psalm-like prayers to be found in the Bible outside the Psalter itself, it is known as a 'canticle' or little song. It is a song of thanksgiving and of joy.

Prayerful Ponderings

'Truly, God is my salvation, I trust, I shall not fear. For the Lord is my strength my song, he became my saviour.'

The singer makes a profession of faith: 'God is my salvation'. The implication is that just as God has saved in the past, so he can be relied upon to do so again. Therefore, declares the singer, 'I trust' him, I put aside my fears. Using the very words that Moses' sister, Miriam, had used at the Exodus (Exodus 15:1-18), the singer addresses the Lord as 'my strength', 'my song' and 'my saviour'. As we await the arrival of our Saviour-God at Christmas, we can, with even greater confidence, declare that for us the Lord is an utterly reliable source of strength, he is an unending song of joy, he is our glorious deliverer.

'With joy you will draw water from the wells of salvation.'

Having spoken of his personal discovery of God's power to save, the singer now invites others to enjoy a similar experience. They are assured that to seek the Lord's assistance is like drawing water from bottomless 'wells' of saving help.

'Give thanks to the Lord, give praise to his name! Make his mighty deeds known to the peoples! Declare the greatness of his name.'

It could only be a matter of time before the singer calls upon everyone who hears him to 'give thanks to the Lord', to 'give [him] praise' and to 'make his mighty deeds known' to people everywhere. Thanksgiving should be a characteristic feature in the lives of all who know of God's 'mighty deeds' and have experienced his 'greatness'.

'Sing a psalm to the Lord for he has done glorious deeds, make them known to all the earth!'

One of the most obvious ways in which we can give thanks is by the singing of 'a psalm to the Lord' – which is of course precisely what we have done in this Sunday's liturgy. However, there is no reason for it to be restricted in that way: throughout the week we might make a special effort to express our gratitude to God, especially in anticipation of the nativity of his Son which we shall soon be celebrating.

'People of Zion, sing and shout for joy for great in your midst is the Holy One of Israel.'

These words form the response to today's psalm/canticle. It was natural for the singer to speak expressly of 'Zion' (Jerusalem) for that is where 'the Holy One', God himself, was believed to dwell 'in [the] midst' of his people. In this season of Advent our thoughts turn naturally to Mary for in her midst is the unborn Child whose coming should have us singing and shouting 'for joy'.

LET US PRAY: *In union with Mary, we pray that our soul may magnify the Lord, that our spirit may rejoice in God our Saviour and that we may be filled with thanksgiving because of the great things he has done for us through Jesus his Son.*

Fourth Sunday
of Advent

Not from mighty Jerusalem, says the prophet Micah (5:1-4), but from lowly Bethlehem will come the Messiah King.

With Christmas now only a few days away, we are reminded (Hebrews 10:5-10) that our Saviour, whose one desire is to do the will of his Father, had a human body like our own and in that body he offered the sacrifice by which we are saved.

King David danced joyously before the ark of the Lord (2 Samuel 6:2-16); the gospel (Luke 1:39-45) tells how the unborn John leaped with joy in the presence of Mary, the new Ark of the Covenant.

Psalm 79 is a plea for help in a time of national disaster, but the verses chosen from the psalm for the day's responsorial psalm are especially those which can be applied to the Messiah King.

Prayerful Ponderings

'God of hosts, bring us back; let your face shine on us and we shall be saved.'
The refrain to the responsorial psalm is an appeal to the 'God of hosts', which is a title referring to the powerful army of heavenly beings that surrounds his heavenly throne (see Isaiah 6:3) and is also associated with the ark of the covenant. The appeal is that he will 'bring us back', that he will restore us to his friendship. The final words of this verse take on a special meaning as we make ready for Christmas: the birth of Jesus is like the brightness of God's smile shining 'on us', and with it comes the promise that 'we shall be saved'.

'O shepherd of Israel, hear us, shine forth from your cherubim throne. O Lord, rouse up your might, O Lord, come to our help.'
'Shepherd of Israel' is a title for God, the king who leads his people out of slavery, protecting and providing for them in all their needs. His throne, the ark of the covenant, was borne by 'cherubim', strange eagle-winged creatures associated with the presence of God in the ancient Middle East. The image these descriptions create is that of an all-powerful God; he is called upon to 'rouse up [his] might' and to 'come to our help'. We know that our Shepherd King will soon come to us, we know that his throne is surrounded by angel hosts, like those that sang above the stable at Bethlehem, we know that he is coming to our help, yet we also know that he will

slip into our world not in the panoply of a warrior but in the body of a tiny child. In today's gospel Elizabeth announces his arrival as she salutes Mary with the cry: 'Blessed is the fruit of your womb.'

'God of hosts, turn again, we implore, look down from heaven and see. Visit this vine and protect it, the vine your right hand has planted.'

Again an appeal to the God of power. It as though God has turned away from his people; hence the appeal that he will 'turn [back to them] again'. This time he is compared to a vinedresser and his people to a 'vine', a vine that was 'planted' by his own 'right hand'. And so he is asked to 'visit' this vine of his and 'protect it'. In these Advent days we too are encouraged, especially in the liturgy, to imagine ourselves in the position of those who lived before the birth of Christ, so that we too earnestly beg that our Saviour may come into our lives.

'May your hand be on the man you have chosen, the man you have given your strength. And we shall never forsake you again: give us life that we may call upon your name.'

The first sentence is a prayer for 'the man you have chosen' and to whom 'you have given your strength'. In its original setting it referred to the anointed (messiah) king who ruled over Israel. At Christmas time we celebrate the way God has 'turned again' to us his people in the person of the anointed one, the Christ, the Messiah King. The final sentence might easily be used as a petition that the coming celebrations will make us strong so that we may 'never forsake you again', that they may bring us fullness of the 'life' of grace that we may eagerly 'call upon your name' in prayer.

LET US PRAY: *We give thanks to you, God our Father, mighty King and loving Shepherd, that you have sent us a Messiah who has come in our humanity so that we may gain a share in his divinity.*

CHRISTMASTIDE

The
Word
became flesh
Alleluia
Alleluia

CHRISTMASTIDE

'The Christ-child lay on Mary's lap,
His hair was like a light.
(O weary, weary were the world,
But here is all aright.)

'The Christ-child lay on Mary's breast
His hair was like a star.
(O stern and cunning are the kings,
But here the true hearts are.)

'The Christ-child lay on Mary's heart,
His hair was like a fire.
(O weary, weary is the world,
But here the world's desire.)

'The Christ-child stood at Mary's knee,
His hair was like a crown,
And all the flowers looked up at Him,
And all the stars looked down.'

(G. K. Chesterton)

The Nativity of Our Lord, Mass during the Day

After the almost magical quality of the Midnight and Dawn Masses, the Mass of Christmas Day may seem more reflective, even more solemn in tone; there is, for example, no account of the birth of Christ. Nonetheless the sound of joy is far from being stifled, above all in the responsorial psalm.

The first reading (Isaiah 52:7-10) takes us back some six centuries before our Lord was born; it tells how good – incredibly good – news will be proclaimed to Israel: its time of exile is over; there is to be peace and happiness, for the Lord God will exert his royal power, and 'all the ends of the earth shall see the salvation of our God'. Psalm 97, another of the Enthronement Psalms and a companion piece to Psalm 96, rejoices that what the prophecy foretold has come to pass.

The second reading (Hebrews 1:1-6) confirms that we have indeed seen God's salvation, and that means the end of our spiritual exile. In former times people were able to catch only a fragmentary glimpse of God through the prophets, but now we see him revealed in the person of his beloved Son. He is the perfect reflection of the Father; through him, the Word, all things came into existence and through him we are set free from 'the defilement of sin'.

The gospel, the golden preface of St John (1:1-18), has the same message: Jesus, God's creative Word who endows everyone with life and light, has now been 'made flesh', bringing into the world a light which nothing can quench and which enables us to see that God has remembered his faithful love.

The Masses for Midnight and Dawn are to be found in volumes Year A and B, respectively

Prayerful Ponderings

'Sing a new song to the Lord for he has worked wonders.'
Very probably this psalm was composed about the same time as today's first reading; it calls for a song of praise to be sung because of the incredible wonder, the 'new thing', that God has worked by releasing his people from exile. Throughout the centuries the Church has taken up the same cry, summoning us to 'sing a new song to the Lord', but this time for the even greater wonder he has worked for us; an altogether new situation has arisen from the fact that 'the Word was made flesh and dwelt among us'.

'His right hand and his holy arm have brought salvation.'
The references to 'hand' and 'arm' suggest the presence of a mighty warrior who in his strength is able to curb all his enemies. Kneeling at the crib, we may find it hard to think in terms of power and might; what can a new-born child accomplish with his meagre strength? And yet this Child is set to topple all our enemies and win us the salvation we long for; his story will vindicate the words of St Paul that 'God's weakness is stronger than human strength', just as his 'foolishness is wiser than human wisdom' (1 Corinthians 1:25).

'The Lord has made known his salvation; has shown his justice to the nations. He has remembered his truth and love for the house of Israel.'
The birth in Bethlehem is the beginning of a story which will

culminate in a cross on Calvary, an empty tomb in Jerusalem, a seat at the right hand of the Father in heaven. Begun in the hiddenness of a cave, it will be broadcast to all the earth. The whole world will learn that God has 'remembered his truth [his steadfastness]' and his covenant 'love'; Mary herself recognises this truth for in her own song, the Magnificat, she proclaims that it is 'in remembrance of his mercy' that God has come to our rescue through his Son, Jesus. As he remembered his promises, so he wants us to remember his saving love.

'All the ends of the earth have seen the salvation of our God. Shout to the Lord all the earth, ring out your joy.'
The first line of this verse ('All the ends ... our God') serves as the response for today's psalm, and fittingly so, for it catches the sense of world-wide rejoicing that runs through the psalm from first verse to last. Since the whole earth has learned of what God has done, the psalmist does not hesitate to call upon it to perform an act of homage, to raise its voice and ring out its joy.

'Sing psalms to the Lord with the harp, with the sound of music. With trumpets and the sound of the horn acclaim the King, the Lord.'
And now various musical instruments are invited to join in the celebration; harps and trumpets and horns are to accompany the songs of praise and to provide an exuberant carol for the Lord. When Isaac Watts came to write his Christmas carol 'Joy to the world, the Lord is come', he found much of his inspiration in this psalm. It is in the birth of Christ, in the coming of the King, that the psalm reaches its truest fulfilment.

LET US PRAY: *Father, you deserve an unending song of praise for the wonders you have done for us in the birth, death and resurrection of your Son, Jesus. On this Christmas Day we beg you to help us as we renew our resolve to praise you with our lips and with our lives.*

The Holy Family of Jesus, Mary and Joseph

On this feast of the Holy Family we are reminded of our status as a pilgrimage people journeying towards our Father's house where the whole family of God will be gathered together.

In the first reading (1 Samuel 1:20-22, 24-28) we see the family of Elkanah and Hannah on pilgrimage to the Temple to thank God for the child who had been granted them in answer to Hannah's prayers.

In the gospel (Luke 2:41-52) it is the Holy Family of Joseph and Mary who are on pilgrimage to the Temple for the feast of Passover; there they experience the tragic 'loss' and then the joyful finding of the Child who is 'busy with my Father's affairs'.

The second reading 1 John 3:1-2, 21-24) speaks about the end of all our pilgrimage journeys – the vision of God and the discovery that we are 'like him because we ... see him as he really is'.

Today's beautiful responsorial psalm, Psalm 83, was used by the people of Israel as they went up, by families, to Jerusalem for the great feasts. Was it, I wonder, sung by the Holy Family, Mary and Joseph and their young son Jesus, as they made their pilgrimage journey to the Temple?

Prayerful Ponderings

'How lovely is your dwelling place, Lord, God of hosts.'
The opening exclamation sets the tone: as the pilgrims approach Jerusalem, they speak of the loveliness of the holy city. However, it is 'lovely' not so much because of its architectural splendour as because of the breath-taking fact that the Temple serves as the 'dwelling place' of the 'Lord, God of hosts', a title specially associated with the ark of the covenant, the principal symbol of the Lord's presence with his people.

'My soul is longing and yearning, is yearning for the courts of the Lord. My heart and my soul ring out their joy to God, the living God.'
The psalmist sings of the 'longing' and the 'yearning for the courts of the Lord' that fill the 'heart' of every pilgrim. However, it isn't simply the temple courts that the pilgrim longs for, but rather 'the living God' himself. He is described as 'living', for, unlike the lifeless gods of the nations, he is both the giver and protector of life, and it is for him that 'heart' and 'soul' alike 'ring out' with 'joy'. Though the Temple and its courts may long since have disappeared, this psalm still has a special significance for us Christians: whenever we go to church, especially for Sunday's liturgy, we are setting out on a kind of pilgrimage, and we do so with a deep-down longing to draw close to the Lord and then a special joy in the realisation of being with him.

'They are happy, who dwell in your house, for ever singing your praise.'

The psalmist thinks of the good fortune of those 'who dwell in your house' and so are able to be involved 'for ever' in 'singing your praise'; does the psalmist have the priests and levites in mind? In any event, they are not merely 'happy' but blessed, in much the same way that the Beatitudes speak of the poor, the meek, those who mourn, etc. as blessed, truly fortunate.

'They are happy, whose strength is in you; they walk with ever growing strength.'

It was tempting, as the previous verse suggests, to envy those who actually dwelt in God's house, just as today it is tempting to envy those groups of enclosed monks and nuns who devote themselves full-time to the praise and service of God. However, the psalmist has another beatitude to speak of: 'happy' also are those 'whose strength is in you'. The reference may be to all the people who are physically on their way to Jerusalem; but it is at least as likely that the psalmist is thinking of all those people who 'walk' in God's ways in the course of their daily lives. The truth is that people who live 'in the world', as Mary and Joseph did, are no less 'happy', no less blessed, than those who live in convents and monasteries. Indeed, they also live in God's house for God dwells in the heart of their homes just as truly as he does in church buildings, and his 'strength' is experienced there, enabling them to walk in his ways.

'O Lord, God of hosts, hear my prayer, give ear, O God of Jacob. Turn your eyes, O God, our shield, look on the face of your anointed.'

Towards the end of the psalm comes this enthusiastic prayer, couched in simple language. It falls into two parts; the first, addressed to the 'Lord, God of hosts' and 'God of Jacob', is in the form of an appeal that God will turn his 'ear', the better to 'hear my prayer'; the second that God, now called 'our shield', will turn his 'eyes', the better to 'look' (with care and concern) 'on the face of your anointed'. The reference here is to the king, the anointed one, upon whom the people are so completely dependent. However, by baptism we are all anointed ones, we all share in the royal – as well as the priestly and prophetic – dignity of the children of God (see second reading); and so this prayer can easily be applied to ourselves.

LET US PRAY: *As we honour the Holy Family, we pray, God our Father and our shield of protection, that every Christian family may be your dwelling place and that parents and children alike may strive to live lives worthy of you.*

Mary, Mother of God

In becoming man, Jesus took upon himself our humanity in its entirety. That meant that he was born in a particular time and place, that he became the member of a particular race, and that, as the gospel recounts, he was circumcised on the octave day of his birth, like any other Jewish male child, (today is the final day of the Christmas Octave).

The first reading (Numbers 6:22-27) consists of an instruction on the blessing to be given by the priests. Was it a similar blessing that Jesus and Mary received when she took him to the Temple to be circumcised? The second reading (Galatians 4:4-7) teaches us that it is through Christ in his humanity, Christ 'born of a woman, born subject to the Law', that God has given us the greatest of all blessings, a sharing in the divine life so that we are enabled to call upon him as 'Abba' (dear Father).

In the first part of the gospel (Luke 2:16-21), the shepherds visit the new-born Christ and worship him, and then go on their way blessing and praising God. The responsorial psalm is part of a thanksgiving prayer, Psalm 66; taking up the theme of the shepherds, it blesses and praises the Lord. Originally it was intended as a thanksgiving for the harvest, indeed it may have been composed for a harvest festival such as the Feast of Tabernacles. Only part of it is used in today's Mass; the explicit reference to harvest is absent, and that is unfortunate because today is the feast of Mary's motherhood, and Jesus, the fruit of her womb, is surely the richest harvest this world has ever witnessed.

Prayerful Ponderings

'God, be gracious and bless us and let your face shed its light
upon us.'
These words are an adaptation of the blessing which, according to
Numbers 26:24-26, Aaron and his sons were to use when they
blessed the people. It is a blessing which the priests had
pronounced over and over again throughout Israel's history. But
never was the whole world blessed so magnificently as it was
through the Divine Motherhood of Mary, for her Son is God's
graciousness, God's blessing, the radiant smile of God's face made
visible.

'So will your ways be known upon earth and all nations learn
your saving help.'
However, it quickly becomes clear that the blessing of the Saviour's
birth is to be spread over the whole earth. The Good News of
Bethlehem is to be taken to all the nations so that everyone will
become aware of the wonderful ways of God and of his readiness
to offer 'saving help' to all who are ready to receive it.

'Let the nations be glad and exult for you rule the world with
justice.'
We Christians, like the Jews before us, find joy in the 'rule' and
kingship of our God, and our prayer is that his 'justice', his

impartiality and fairness, may be experienced by our brothers and sisters everywhere.

'With fairness you rule the peoples, you guide the nations on earth.'
It was always Israel's prayer that their earthly king would function as shepherd of his people; his task was not simply to 'rule', but also to 'guide': power and strength were to merge with tenderness and concern for those in his care. In Jesus we find just such a king; his is 'a kingdom of truth and life, a kingdom of holiness and grace, a kingdom of justice, love and peace' (Preface for the feast of Christ the King).

'Let the peoples praise you, O God; let all the peoples praise you.'
This psalm has links with two great Old Testament prophecies. The first is God's promise to Abraham that he will be blessed and then in his turn will be a blessing to all the families of the earth (Genesis 12:1-4). The second is the prophecy to be found in Isaiah 40-55 that the salvation of Israel will be a revelation to all the nations that the Lord reigns and will lead them to praise him. In both cases Israel is the bridgehead by which God's blessing spreads throughout the world. It is through the Church, the 'sacrament' or effective sign of God's salvation, that the whole world is to be drawn to praise him.

'May God still give us his blessing till the ends of the earth revere him.'
The responsorial psalm ends with this appeal that God will continue to favour us with such blessings that we in our turn may prove to be blessing to 'the ends of the earth' – to everyone everywhere.

LET US PRAY: *Lord, we thank you for the harvest of blessings we have received from you, and above all for your dear Son, Jesus, born of the Virgin Mary. We beg you to continue to bless us day by day so that we may bear witness to you unceasingly and others may thereby be drawn to you.*

Second Sunday after Christmas

Psalm 147 was composed for the congregation of Jerusalem which, after long years in exile, had returned home and set about restoring city and Temple. The people were filled with a desire to praise God for they knew that the reversal of fortune was due to God's intervention: that it was he who enabled them to rejoice once more in Jerusalem, to experience peace, to enjoy plentiful harvests; and that it was he who blessed them with his words and decrees.

At Christmastide – Christmas Day is still only a short time ago – we too are encouraged to raise our voices in praise as we recall all the good things that have come our way, thanks to the birth and life of Jesus. He has 'pitched his tent among us' (see the first reading [Ecclesiasticus 24:1-2, 8-12] and the gospel [John 1:1-18]); he has destroyed our alienation from God, raising us to dizzy heights as the adopted children of God (see the second reading [Ephesians 1:3-6, 15-18]); and he has drawn us into the 'Jerusalem' of his Church.

Prayerful Ponderings

'The Word was made flesh, and lived among us.'
These words are not, of course, part of the psalm – they come from St John's Gospel – but they are an admirable response to the psalm when viewed through Christian eyes. Our supreme reason for making this song of praise our own is that God has come to us in the person of Jesus Christ: he, the Word, the almighty Son of God, has taken upon himself our human condition and the consequences are wonderful beyond anything we could imagine.

'O praise the Lord, Jerusalem! Zion, praise your God!'
In the psalms the word 'Jerusalem' does not always refer to the city of that name; sometimes it means all the citizens, or even the whole people of God. And today we, God's people, pray this psalm to praise God for what he has done in building the 'new Jerusalem', his Church (which is itself a foretaste of the new Jerusalem of heaven) and for upholding it amidst all the eventualities of history.

'He has strengthened the bars of your gates, he has blessed the children within you.'
When the exiles returned, they had to look to the defence of their city; sturdy wooden bars ensured that when the city gates were closed they were secure. Within that security the people could again grow in numbers, after the terrible losses they had sustained.

Nonetheless, they saw within and above their activities the loving care of God for his people. As we pray this psalm we too thank God for the care he lavishes on his Church, ensuring that 'the gates of hell will not prevail against it' and blessing it in every age with new children in the sacrament of baptism.

'He established peace on your borders, he feeds you with finest wheat.'

This is another line which takes on richer meaning when applied to the Church, whose peace and essential unity God preserves despite scandals and setbacks and divisions. Above all, the Lord feeds us with 'finest wheat' – himself in the Holy Eucharist – and the first purpose of Holy Communion is to build up a common-union of love first with him and then with one another.

'He sends out his word to the earth and swiftly runs his command. He makes his word known to Jacob, to Israel his laws and decrees.'

The 'laws and decrees' given by God to his covenant people (Jacob/Israel) were seen as a revelation of his will and therefore as a precious gift. The distinguishing feature of this people was the fact that God had spoken to them, they had heard his word. And in the Church we rejoice in God's word, the Scriptures through which he reveals himself to us, and, above all, in his Word (with a capital W) whose birthday we are now celebrating and whose teaching is our joy.

'He has not dealt thus with other nations; he has not taught them his decrees.'

Israel rejoiced in the singular gifts that God had bestowed upon them. It was only with the passage of time that they began to realise that God's gifts, in particular his revelation, were not just for them but for the whole human race. There is no excuse for us Christians, however, if we do not recognise the universal implications of our Lord's coming. His last word to his disciples was that they should go forth and teach all nations, baptising all who would believe and bringing them into the bosom of the Church.

LET US PRAY: *We thank and praise you, Lord, for the gifts that you have bestowed upon us so generously. We ask you to keep your family in your peace and continue to sustain us with the bread of the Eucharist that we may be filled with a sense of security and of hope.*

The Epiphany
of the Lord

The Epiphany is one of the oldest Christian feasts. It is not only older than Christmas, but also has a deeper significance, for rather than celebrating simply the birth of Christ, it also celebrates the whole purpose of his incarnation – the 'epiphany', that is, the appearance, or manifestation, of God through his Son, Jesus. And so it serves as a fitting culmination to the Christmas season.

Today's first reading (Isaiah 60:1-6) is full of optimism: the people will be brought back home from exile and Jerusalem, once restored, will manifest the Lord to all peoples, drawing them from darkness into glorious light. Paul (Ephesians 3:2-3, 5-6) takes up a similar theme: the secret at the heart of Christianity is that all peoples, Jews and non-Jews alike, are called to be members of the one Body of which Jesus is the Head.

Today's gospel (Matthew 2:1-12) also bears witness to the universal character of the 'good news', for it tells of the visit of the Magi, probably practitioners in the occult arts, who come from far-away lands with gifts – it seems that the practice of gift-giving at Christmastide arose from this episode – for the new-born King.

The responsorial psalm, taken from Psalm 71 with the response 'All nations shall fall prostrate before you, O Lord', chimes in well with the other readings: the Messiah King will be worshipped by all peoples, he will be reverenced and plied with gifts even by kings from distant lands.

Prayerful Ponderings

'O God, give your judgement to the king, to a king's son your justice, that he may judge your people in justice and your poor in right judgement.'

In all probability this psalm was composed for the coronation of a Davidic king in Jerusalem, but it is a portrait so utopian that no one could ever live up to its incredible ideals except that Messianic king who was born in the humble setting of a stable. He, as we know, is not merely the 'king's son', but the Son of the King of kings. That is why he can be relied upon to reflect 'your justice', a justice worthy of God himself, and to show a special concern for the poor, for they are God's poor ('your poor').

'In his days justice shall flourish and peace till the moon fails. He shall rule from sea to sea, from the Great River to earth's bounds.'

His reign, bringing with it 'justice' and every kind of well-being (*shalom*), will endure for ever – even 'till the moon fails', as the psalmist quaintly puts it. Just as the king's reign is endless, so his realm is boundless, 'from sea to sea', an expression which may refer to the promised boundaries of the holy land, from 'the Great River' of the Euphrates to the sea of the Mediterranean, or to the ancient notion that the earth was like an island in the midst of waters, so that 'from sea to sea' would be equivalent to from east to west.

'The kings of Tarshish and the sea coasts shall pay him tribute. The kings of Sheba and Seba shall bring him gifts. Before him all kings shall fall prostrate, all nations shall serve him.'

Whatever the precise location of 'Tarshish and the sea coasts' – the reference is perhaps to Spain – the expression is certainly meant to underline the fact that it is from the ends of the earth that kings come to acknowledge the King. There seems little doubt that in his account of the Magi's visit, Matthew had in mind the psalmist's reference to gift-bearing 'kings of Sheba and Seba'. A queen of Sheba once arrived in Jerusalem laden with gifts for King Solomon (1 Kings 10), but there is 'a greater than Solomon' here in the stable of Bethlehem.

'For he shall save the poor when they cry and the needy who are helpless. He will have pity on the weak and save the lives of the poor.'

Once more it is made clear that the long-awaited King will be full of compassion; he will have a special concern for 'the poor', 'the needy' and 'the weak'; indeed, he will have practical experience of the lot of the poor.

LET US PRAY: *On this day of Christmastide, we give thanks to you, Lord, for drawing us into the kingdom of your Son and enabling us to see in him the most perfect revelation of yourself. Like the Magi, may we bow low before him, offering the precious gifts of our faith, our hope and our love.*

The Baptism of the Lord

An anonymous prophet of the sixth century is responsible for the section of Isaiah (40:1-5, 9-11) from which today's first reading comes. It offers words of consolation to the people in exile: God will restore them in what will be a second exodus, the holy city will announce his coming and he will care for his people as a shepherd cares for his flock.

In the gospel (Luke 3:15-16, 21-22) John the Baptist announces the coming of the Messiah. As Jesus is baptised, the Father acknowledges him as his beloved Son; it is through him that a still greater exodus will take place: through his death and resurrection we will be led to the promised land of heaven.

The letter to Titus (2:11-14; 3:4-7) reveals what Christ's coming means – 'the kindness and love of God' revealed, 'salvation for the whole human race', 'the cleansing water of rebirth' (baptism) made available to us and the gift of 'the Holy Spirit' poured out upon us.

Psalm 103, from which today's responsorial psalm comes, is a paean of praise for God's wonderful work of creation. It also offers us words with which to thank him for the still greater wonders worked in us through the re-creation brought about by baptism.

Prayerful Ponderings

'Bless the Lord, my soul! Lord God, how great you are!'
An outburst of praise, as the psalmist calls upon 'my soul' (my whole self) to 'bless the Lord', to rejoice in him and all his creation. The wonder aroused by the sight of what God has done leads to an exclamation of awe and astonishment, which in its turn sums up what this psalm is about from start to finish: 'Lord God, how great you are!' It's a cry that is taken up time and time again as part of the refrain of today's responsorial psalm.

'Lord God, how great you are, clothed in majesty and glory, wrapped in light as in a robe!'
Again the exclamation of wonder at the greatness of our God. He is visualised as a mighty King. However, his regal robes, unlike those of earthly monarchs, are fashioned of the sheer 'majesty and glory' of his being, and he is 'wrapped in light' as though clothed with a royal cloak.

'You stretch out the heavens like a tent. Above the heavens you build your dwelling. You make the clouds your chariot, you walk on the wings of the wind, you make the winds your messengers and flashing fire your servants.'
From the King's attire to the King's activities. Like a nomad putting up his tent in the desert, the Lord stretches out the tent-cloth of

'the heavens'. It usually took a couple of people to pitch a tent, but he is able to do it on his own and, it would seem, effortlessly. His own 'dwelling' is hidden away 'above the heavens', and he is depicted as using 'the clouds' as a 'chariot' on which to visit his domain. The creatures of the heavens are like his courtiers: 'the winds', mysterious in their origin and purpose, are his 'messengers' while the lightnings of 'flashing fire' are his 'servants'.

'How many are your works, O Lord! In wisdom you have made them all. The earth is full of your riches. There is the sea, vast and wide, with its moving swarms past counting, living things great and small.'

From the heavens, the psalmist's gaze turns, first, towards 'the earth' – that too is filled with God's created 'riches' – and, then, towards 'the sea', so 'vast and wide', with countless shoals of 'moving', 'living' creatures, some large, some 'small'. And the psalmist, almost lost for words, can only praise the 'wisdom' of God's work and murmur in awe: 'How many are your works, O Lord'

'All of these look to you to give them their food in due season. You give it, they gather it up: you open your hand, they have their fill.'

Not only is God the creator of all that is, he is also the provider for everything that is. It is he who ensures 'food' for human and beast alike; he is the giver, they the gatherers; he is the benefactor opening a 'hand' that is filled with generous gifts, they the recipients, receiving from him all that they need.

'You take back your spirit, they die, returning to the dust from which they came. You send forth your spirit, they are created; and you renew the face of the earth.'

Finally the recognition that God's creative work is ongoing; it is his 'spirit', and the breath that he breathes into them, that continues to keep his creatures alive. Whenever and wherever 'the face of the earth' is renewed and new life springs into being, there the creative spirit of the Lord is at work. Of course all this takes on a new and dazzling significance in the spiritual order: at our baptism the Holy Spirit, breathed out in love between Father and Son, came to make his home within us and we became 'a new creation'.

LET US PRAY: *O God, our creator and most generous benefactor, we thank you for all the wonders of creation that we discover in the heavens, on the earth and in the seas; but above all we thank you for the wonders of your spiritual creation in our souls.*

LENT

By
his sufferings
shall
my servant
justify
many

LENT

'This hour of grace thou dost impart;
Teach us with flowing tears the stain
To cleanse from every victim-heart
That longs to feel love's welcome pain.

'The day is come, the accepted day,
When grace like nature flowers anew;
Trained by thy hand the surer way
Rejoice we in our spring-time too.'
(sixth-century hymn translated by R. A. Knox)

First Sunday of Lent

The first readings of the Sundays of Lent call to mind major stages of salvation history. Today we have an outline of that history, from the time when God's people 'went down into Egypt' to the time when they entered the Promised Land.

The gospel (Luke 4:1-13) recounts the first stage in Jesus' saving ministry: in the desert he faces the 'tempter', who though defeated will 'return at the appointed time' (the time of the Passion).

The first reading (Deuteronomy 26:4-10) is in the form of a creed recited at a harvest festival; the second reading (Romans 10:8-13) is a baptismal creed promising salvation to whoever confesses with their lips that Jesus is Lord and believes in their hearts that God raised him from the dead.

Psalm 90, which provides the verses for today's responsorial psalm, is a classic example of a psalm of confidence in God. In the words of St Athanasius: 'If you desire ... to know what confidence is to be reposed in God, and what makes the mind fearless, you will praise God by reciting the ninetieth Psalm' (quoted by James L. Mays).

Prayerful Ponderings

'He who dwells in the shelter of the Most High and abides in the shade of the Almighty says to the Lord: "My refuge, my stronghold, my God in whom I trust!"'

The psalm begins with a confession of faith which is meant to serve also as an exhortation to others to trust in God. As one 'who dwells in the shelter of the Most High and abides in the shade of the Almighty' – presumably, a reference to his serving as a minister in the temple precincts -- the psalmist boldly proclaims his conviction that the Lord is security and protection from every danger: he is not merely a 'refuge' and a 'stronghold' and a 'God in whom [to] trust', but *my* refuge, *my* stronghold, *my* God in whom I trust. If the repeated emphasis on the possessive 'my' speaks of the intimacy of the relationship, the four different words used of the Other Partner in that relationship indicates that he is the utterly transcendent One. He is 'the Most High' (Elyon), a title which suggests that he is beyond compare; he is 'the Almighty' (Shaddai), the title by which he was known to the Patriarchs; he is Lord (Yahweh), the name associated with Moses and the Exodus; he is 'God' (Elohim), who has been trusted throughout the ages.

'Upon you no evil shall fall, no plague approach where you dwell. For you he has commanded his angels to keep you in all your ways.'

It would be dangerous to infer from these words, or from those of the following verses, that believers will be untouched by adversity. On the contrary they are the assurance that even when adversity strikes, it will not undermine their faith in God's providence. He has put them under the care of mighty 'angels to keep [them] in all [their] ways' and nothing 'shall befall' us without our Father knowing (see Matthew 6:25-34), and though they may have to face 'hardship, or distress, or persecution, or famine...', yet 'all things work together for good for those who love God' (Romans 8:35 and 28).

'They shall bear you upon their hands lest you strike your foot against a stone. On the lion and the viper you will tread and trample the young lion and the dragon.'
After the initial call to trust in the Lord, the psalmist lists a series of threats and dangers that will be encountered – and surmounted – on the journey through life. There is the assurance that God's angels will look after us though we have to face the various adversities symbolised by fierce animals like 'the lion', deadly ones like 'the viper' and fantastic ones like 'the dragon'! It was of course this verse which Satan twisted to his own ends in his temptation of Jesus (see today's gospel); Jesus' response was to reaffirm his absolute trust in the Father. Genuine trust never means putting God to the test by taking unwarranted risks.

'His love he set on me, so I will rescue him; protect him for he knows my name. When he calls I shall answer: "I am with you." I will save him in distress and give him glory.'
At this point, there is an exciting development: suddenly we hear

the direct speech of God himself. In answer to the prayer of loving trust on the part of the believer – 'his love he set on me' – God now responds with these wonderful promises: 'I will rescue him', 'protect him', 'answer him', 'save him' and finally 'give him glory'. When we express a genuine trust in God, it is always he that has the last word.

LET US PRAY: *Lord, when times are difficult and it's hard to trust in you, may this beautiful psalm renew our confidence. Whatever may happen, may we have the courage to pray: 'Be with me, Lord, in my distress', and to believe that the prayer is answered.*

Second Sunday of Lent

This week's first reading (Genesis 15:5-12, 17-18) draws attention to another important stage of salvation history: God makes a covenant with Abraham, promising him many descendants and a land of their own.

If the first reading was hope-filled, the gospel (Luke 9:28-36) radiates a still more spectacular hope, for the transfiguration brings with it the prospect of eternal glory.

The second reading, from the letter to the Philippians (3:17-4:1), speaks of the hope that all Christians have as we wait in eager longing for the coming of the Lord and our own entrance into glory.

Once again this Sunday's psalm, taken from Psalm 26, is a song of confident trust, the kind of trust that must have inspired Abraham (see first reading). Still more it inspired Jesus who at his transfiguration was speaking to Moses and Elijah about his forthcoming death (see the gospel).

Prayerful Ponderings

'**The Lord is my light and my help; whom shall I fear? The Lord is the stronghold of my life; before whom shall I shrink?**'
From the outset the psalmist's position is made clear: with 'the Lord' as 'my light', 'my help' and 'the stronghold of my life' whom is there to 'fear', from what should 'I shrink' back? The Lord is a light that no darkness can extinguish (Jesus, the revelation of the Father, is the Light of the world, a light that darkness did not, and cannot, overcome [John 1:5]; at the transfiguration that light shone in all its brilliance). The Lord is a help that will never fail us. The Lord is a stronghold that can never be destroyed.

'**O Lord, hear my voice when I call; have mercy and answer. Of you my heart has spoken: "Seek his face."**'
A lengthy profession of trust – only part of it appears in today's responsorial psalm – serves as preparation for an appeal to God for help. '[H]ear my voice when I call' is the earnest cry of the psalmist. The vagueness in the wording of the plea - 'have mercy and answer' – means that this prayer is easily adaptable to any trial or difficulty we might encounter. Whatever our troubles, the advice coming from the psalmist's 'heart' is: 'seek [the] face' of the Lord. Seeking the face of the Lord was a consecrated phrase for journeying to the Temple in order to invoke divine help. Of course even that journey is not necessary for, in the words of another psalm, the Lord 'is close to all who call him, who call on him from their hearts' (Psalm 144:18).

'It is your face, O Lord, that I seek; hide not your face. Dismiss not your servant in anger; you have been my help.'

Once more the psalmist appeals for the Lord's presence. The Lord's 'face' is always directed towards us and yet there are times when it feels so different, it seems that he has turned away from us, and we join the psalmist in pleading 'hide not your face'. If such a calamity were to happen it would mean that I, 'your servant', would have been dismissed – the result of your 'anger'. Then, with the psalmist, we correct ourselves by once more expressing trust: the Lord has always 'been my help', and he will be my help still.

'I am sure I shall see the Lord's goodness in the land of the living. Hope in him, hold firm and take heart. Hope in the Lord!'

Fortified by renewal of trust in the Lord, the psalmist speaks confidently of what the future holds in store – an experience of 'the Lord's goodness' throughout life. It may be that the psalmist was sick and 'the land of the living' refers to restoration to good health. The eyes of Christian faith are able to look beyond any tragedy, even death itself. At his trial in 1586 Francis Ingleby, the Yorkshire martyr, recited these very words, when it became clear that he would be executed.

LET US PRAY: *We pray that we may always seek your face with confidence, Lord, for you are our light, our help and our stronghold. In all life's eventualities may we hope in you, hold firm and take heart, hope in you, the Lord, confident that we shall see your goodness in the land of eternal life.*

Third Sunday of Lent

Today's first reading (Exodus 3:1-8, 13-15) brings us to the third stage of salvation history; the call of Moses and the revelation to him of God's sacred name.

The fate which befell many of Moses' people in the desert, says St Paul (1 Corinthians 10:1-6, 10-12), should serve as a warning to us: baptism is in itself no guarantee against temptation or against the possibility of sin; we too must be careful that we do not fail.

In today's gospel (Luke 13:1-9) we hear Jesus' call to repentance; he also speaks of the enduring patience of God and, by way of illustration, tells the parable about the sterile fig tree which is given yet another chance of bearing fruit.

Psalm 102, from which the verses of today's responsorial psalm are taken, is a hymn of deepest gratitude to God for the divine patience and mercy which the psalmist has experienced.

Prayerful Ponderings

'My soul, give thanks to the Lord, all my being, bless his holy name. My soul give thanks to the Lord and never forget all his blessings.'

Psalms of praise and gratitude are usually in the form of a call to others to join the psalmist in thanking God, but this time the opening words of the psalm are addressed to 'my soul', to the psalmist's own innermost self. It seems to be an emphatic way of saying: I will 'give thanks to the Lord', I myself will 'bless his holy name'; but of course today we are meant to make the psalmist's words of praise our own. Nor is it to be a mere outward show: it must involve 'all my being'. I must never allow myself to become unmindful of the countless 'blessings' I receive from God: an ungrateful Christian sounds like a contradiction in terms.

'It is he who forgives all your guilt, who heals every one of your ills, who redeems your life from the grave, who crowns you with love and compassion.'

The particular blessing for which the psalmist wishes to give thanks on this occasion is God's endless mercy and forgiveness. A series of verbs, coming one after the other, helps to create a picture of the extraordinary generosity of the Lord; if my praise involves 'all my being' (see previous verse) so also God's loving mercy affects me in every aspect of my being: he 'forgives', he 'heals', he 'redeems', he 'crowns'. God's forgiveness is a permanent sign that I am always encompassed by God's 'love and compassion', his covenant faithfulness.

'The Lord does deeds of justice, gives judgement for all who are oppressed. He made known his ways to Moses and his deeds to Israel's sons.'

Not content with thanking God for personal favours, the psalmist goes on to thank him for all his saving acts, his 'deeds of justice', on behalf of his people, beginning with his calling of 'Moses' and the entrusting to him of his own sacred name (see first reading), his guidance and protection of 'Israel's sons' during the desert days and beyond, and, in a special way, the concern he has always shown for the 'oppressed', those who experience need of any kind. As Christians we remember with gratitude the still more wonderful 'deeds of justice' which have been worked for us by Christ and which he continues to work through his mystical Body, the Church.

'The Lord is compassion and love, slow to anger and rich in mercy. For as the heavens are high above the earth so strong is his love for those who fear him.'

It is hardly surprising that the first words of this verse – 'The Lord is compassion and love' – serve as the refrain for the responsorial psalm, for they highlight the major theme of today's readings: our God does not merely show compassion and love; he IS compassion and love: that is his very nature. It is a love and compassion which tower as 'high above' us as 'the heavens are high above the earth'. Of course God is not indifferent to evil – if he were, he would be indifferent to goodness too – and the psalmist tries to reflect this notion by speaking of God's 'anger'. However, he insists that his anger is 'slow', not easily aroused, and, even when it is, the richness of his 'mercy' is in no way diminished.

LET US PRAY: *Each Lent, Lord God, we are challenged to repent, to seek — while there is still time — your boundless mercy; help us to respond generously to your call and so to experience your forgiveness.*

Fourth Sunday of Lent

Another significant stage of salvation history: at last the people of Israel reach the Promised Land, the Passover feast is celebrated, they no longer need the heaven-sent food, the manna, which had nourished them during their desert wanderings (Joshua 5:9-12).

In response to those who criticise him for eating with 'sinners', Jesus tells the unforgettable parable of the wastrel son who was received back so magnanimously by his father. It's a parable which provides an insight into the love and compassion of our heavenly Father (Luke 15:1-3, 11-32)

Paul reminds us that in his own person Jesus is the reconciliation between us and God; his whole life is an expression of the mission on which the Father sent him (2 Corinthians 5:17-21).

The verses from Psalm 33 which form this Sunday's psalm are in the form of a prayer of gratitude for having been enabled to savour the goodness of the Lord.

Prayerful Ponderings

'Taste and see that the Lord is good.'

This is the refrain of today's psalm. In the first reading we heard how God provided food for his people when they were in need. In bidding us to 'taste and see that the Lord is good', the psalmist has much more than physical eating in mind; the invitation is to experience the Lord's goodness in all its aspects, to savour his boundless mercy (see gospel), to rejoice in his provision of our daily needs. St Peter (1 Peter 2:3) refers to this verse in speaking of the work of our salvation: we ought to exult in the reconciliation which Jesus has won for us and to relish the prospect of eating with him in the banquet of heaven. Not surprisingly, such 'tasting' of the Lord's goodness leads to thankful praise.

'I will bless the Lord at all times, his praise always on my lips; in the Lord my soul shall make its boast. The humble shall hear and be glad.'

Just as God's goodness is permanent, affecting us 'at all times', so it is anticipated that we shall 'bless' him 'at all times', that 'his praise' will be constantly 'on [our] lips' and that we shall make him our 'boast'. In the words of Paul, we should 'give thanks in all circumstances' (1 Thessalonians 5:18). Like the repentant sinner in the gospel, it is especially 'the humble', those who know their need of mercy, who will most readily 'hear' the psalmist's words and 'be glad' to respond to them.

'Glorify the Lord with me. Together let us praise his name. I sought the Lord and he answered me; from all my terrors he set me free.'

The psalmist has had personal experience of God's goodness: at a time of great difficulty or more probably of great danger, he 'sought the Lord' and his prayer was 'answered': 'from all my terrors [the Lord] set me free'. And so he urges us to join him in praising 'his name'; come, he says, 'glorify the Lord with me'.

'Look towards him and be radiant; let your faces not be abashed. This poor man called the Lord heard him and rescued him from all his distress.'

Again a personal testimony: the psalmist speaks of himself as a 'poor man' who cried out to 'the Lord' in his time of need and who was 'rescued... from all his distress'. He begs his hearers to join him in looking towards the Lord so that the psalmist's own experience may also be theirs. The realisation that 'God made [Jesus] the sinless one into sin, so that in him we might become the goodness of God' (second reading) should make us 'radiant' with joy and gratitude.

LET US PRAY: *God our Father, we have tasted your goodness, above all in your sending us your Son so that in him we might become a new creation. May our response be one of constant gratitude and may our lives bear witness to the re-creation you have worked in us.*

Fifth Sunday of Lent

Another key event in salvation history was God's restoration of Israel after the years of exile in Babylon. Isaiah (43:16-21) likens that restoration to a second Exodus, with God opening a way to freedom through the sea.

The theme of restoration is highlighted by today's responsorial psalm. Psalm 125 is one of the Songs of Ascent, sung as the pilgrims made their way to Jerusalem. It recalls the joy experienced by the exiles as they returned home.

The gospel (John 8:1-11) tells the story of accusers who look only for condemnation of the adulteress; but it is the joy of restoration that is offered her by Jesus.

Paul is always vividly aware of 'the supreme advantage of knowing Jesus Christ my Lord'. Yet he also knows that we are in constant need of being restored, and so he strains ahead 'for what is still to come' (Philippians 3:8-14).

Prayerful Ponderings

'When the Lord delivered Zion from bondage, it seemed like a dream. Then was our mouth filled with laughter, on our lips there were songs.'

The pilgrims – this is the seventh of the fifteen 'pilgrim songs' – raise their voices to recall with gratitude the way 'the Lord delivered Zion from bondage' in times gone by. The restoration had been so unexpected, and yet so long desired, that when it did happen it had 'seemed like a dream': they were scarcely able to believe what was taking place. It was an unbelievably joyous time, a time of 'songs' and of 'laughter'.

'The heathens themselves said: "What marvels the Lord worked for them!" What marvels the Lord worked for us! Indeed we were glad.'

Even 'the heathens' had to admit that the restoration ranked as one of the 'marvels' worked by the Lord for his people. And as for the people themselves, they could only agree with them! On this Sunday when, in the refrain to the psalm, we repeat the same cry of joy over and over again – 'What marvels the Lord worked for us! Indeed we were glad' – we realise that we have better reason to rejoice and give thanks than did those who first sang this song, for a still more wonderful restoration has been achieved for us and for the whole human race through the life, death and resurrection of Jesus Christ. Indeed, we are glad.

'Deliver us, O Lord, from our bondage as streams in dry land.'
Memory of the past restoration emboldens the pilgrims to pray
that the restoring work of God may be experienced again in the
present. They beg that the current painful situation – we have no
means of knowing the precise nature of the 'bondage' – may be
changed, just as 'dry land' is transformed when the rains come and
the flowers appear.

'Those who are sowing in tears will sing when they reap.
They go out, they go out, full of tears, carrying seed for the
sowing; they come back, they come back, full of song, carrying
their sheaves.'

Using another analogy, they pray that their present troubles may be
like the time of 'sowing' that is followed by the harvest. In ancient
times when work in the fields was done largely by hand, 'sowing'
may not exactly have reduced farmers to 'tears' but it was certainly
back-breaking work, and it was often, literally, with singing that the
harvest was brought in. The psalmist elaborates the idea with lines
which contrast the outward journey when they are 'full of tears,
carrying seed for the sowing' and the return journey when they are
'full of song, carrying their sheaves'. The repetition of phrases –
'they go out, they go out' and 'they come back, they come back' –
seems to capture the rhythm of the work.

LET US PRAY: *Lord of the harvest, we pray that the sowing we do
through our Lenten exercises may be rewarded with a rich Easter harvest
and, as we renew our baptismal promises, so may we be restored and
renewed as your sons and daughters.*

Passion Sunday

It is hardly surprising that the verses of Psalm 21 which feature in the Mass of Passion Sunday (Palm Sunday) also appear in Masses during Holy Week: they offer us vivid reminders of our Lord's sufferings as well as the first glimmers of his Easter glory.

The psalm itself might have been composed for the mysterious 'disciple' – his identity is not revealed – whom we meet in today's gospel in a passage from Isaiah (50:4-7). There are three similar passages in the second section of Isaiah and all four are commonly referred to as 'Servant Songs', for they speak of a disciple who is the utterly faithful servant of the Lord, who suffers much without offering resistance and whose sufferings bring light and life to his people.

A key to the interpretation of the 'disciple' is to be found in St Paul's wonderful hymn in his letter to the Philippians (2:6-11), where Jesus is presented as one who though divine was the obedient servant of the Father and 'emptied himself' even to death on a cross, and so it is that he has been exalted and is now recognised by all as Lord.

Finally, today's gospel gives us St Luke's account of the passion and death of the Lord (Luke 22:14-23:56). In his typically gentle way, Luke tends to play down the indignities suffered by his Master, as though unable to bear to recall the shameful way he was treated; he stresses Jesus' innocence; he does not highlight the cowardice of the apostles: if they fall asleep, it is through 'sheer grief'; if Peter betrays him, yet the look of Jesus brings him to repentance. But even the 'scribe of the gentleness of Christ' cannot hide the horror of the death and, like the other gospel writers, makes use of Psalm 21 to tell his story.

Prayerful Ponderings

'My God, my God, why have you forsaken me?'
These words, the response for today's psalm, are taken from the opening verse of Psalm 21. They suggest that the psalm is peculiarly relevant to the passion story, for, according to Matthew (27:46), they were upon Jesus' lips as he hung upon the cross, a terrible cry of dereliction, as though he felt himself alienated even from his beloved Abba (dear Father). It is a cry that re-echoes the anguished 'Why?' of all men and women who are bewildered by their suffering. It is a cry that helps us to appreciate how completely our Saviour has 'emptied himself' for our sake. Indeed St Paul says that he 'became a curse for us' (Galatians 3:13).

'All who see me deride me. They curl their lips, they toss their heads. "He trusted in the Lord, let him save him; let him release him if this is his friend."'
The early verses of the psalm depict the sufferer, now placing his complete trust in God, now complaining that God does nor respond. He gazes down upon the upturned faces that surround

him. He has become an object of derision to those who conspired to bring about his death; he notes the cynical curling of 'their lips', the dismissive 'toss [of] their heads'; he hears the almost unbearable taunt: if you really did trust in God, really were his friend, then he would surely intervene on your behalf (see Matthew 27:43–44). But God remains silent. The passion continues.

'Many dogs have surrounded me, they tear holes in my hands and my feet. I can count every one of my bones.'
The middle section of the psalm reads like a nightmare: enemies appear in the guise of salivating 'dogs' and other fearful animals, waiting to tear him to pieces. Already 'hands' and 'feet' have been split open to provide a pathway for the nails of crucifixion. He has become so disfigured and emaciated that as his glance runs down his body he can count his very 'bones', protruding through the flesh.

'They divide my clothing among them. They cast lots for my robe. O Lord, do not leave me alone, my strength, make haste to help me!'
A particularly painful aspect of his suffering is the shame and humiliation it brings. For this most noble and sensitive of men, how degrading to be stripped naked! But that is of no concern to the executioners, who are intent only upon seizing his 'robe', their bonus for a job well done. It is at this moment that the victim calls out once again to the Lord; even now he begs him 'do not leave me alone', even now he has confidence enough to call upon him as 'my strength' and to plead with him to 'make haste to help me'.

'I will tell of your name to my brethren and praise you where they are assembled. "You who fear the Lord give him praise; all sons of Jacob, give him glory. Revere him, Israel's sons."'

The third part of the psalm, from which this verse is taken, is the most unexpected part of all. The Suffering Servant has become the Conquering Victor: in the midst of his anguish, he confidently asserts that he will proclaim God's goodness wherever 'my brethren ... are assembled'. It is difficult to listen to these words and not to think of the glory of the resurrection. Psalm 21 is not simply a cry of anguish but ultimately a hymn of praise to God who brings victory out of defeat. He is the God whom we shall 'fear' (reverence) and 'praise' and glorify as Good Friday gives way to Easter Sunday.

LET US PRAY: *O King of the Friday*
Whose limbs were stretched on the cross,
O Lord, who didst suffer
The bruises, the wounds, the loss,
We stretch ourselves
Beneath the shade of thy might,
Some fruit from the tree of thy passion
Fall on us this night.
(From the Irish)

EASTERTIDE

*This
is the day
which was made
by the Lord:
let us
rejoice*

EASTERTIDE

'This joyful Eastertide
away with sin and sorrow,
my love, the Crucified,
hath sprung to life this morrow:

'Had Christ, that once was slain,
ne'er burst his three-day prison,
our faith had been in vain:
but now hath Christ arisen.'

(George R. Woodward)

Easter Sunday

Today we arrive at the oldest of the Church's feast days and the pinnacle of the Church's liturgical year, the joyful celebration of the resurrection of our Lord Jesus Christ.

The gospel (John 20:1-9) records how the disciples Peter and John slowly came to the realisation that their Master had truly risen. Up to the moment when they stood in the empty tomb and gazed down upon linen cloths, no longer shrouding his body but lying discarded on the ground, they had simply 'failed to understand ... that he must rise from the dead'.

However, as the first reading (Acts 10:34, 37-43) indicates, Peter was later able to proclaim not simply that God had 'raised [Jesus] to life' but that he and the other disciples had actually 'eaten and drunk with him after his resurrection from the dead'.

Each of the alternative second readings – the one taken from Colossians (3:1-4), the other from 1 Corinthians (5:6-8) – draws practical conclusions for all who, through baptism, share in the resurrection. Their new 'life ... is hidden with Christ in God', and therefore their thoughts must no longer be anchored to this earth, they must rid themselves of 'the old yeast', the old way of life.

And finally all is brought together in Psalm 117, THE Easter psalm above all others. The verses for today's Mass are identical with those used at the Vigil Mass; and there will be many reminders of the psalm throughout the Easter season.

Prayerful Ponderings

'This day was made by the Lord; we rejoice and are glad.'
This sentence, which actually belongs to a later verse in Psalm 117, not only serves as response to the psalm but also helps to set the tone for today's great feast. In fact it will be used for the Alleluia verse every day throughout the Easter Octave. Again and again we confess that this astounding day, which sees the resurrection of Jesus from the tomb, is the work of God himself. Only he could have brought it about, only he could even have envisaged such a wonder. And we, who only a few days ago were lamenting the death of Jesus, now find ourselves rejoicing and filled with gladness.

'Give thanks to the Lord for he is good, for his love has no end. Let the sons of Israel say: "His love has no end."'
This is the opening verse of the psalm; its first sentence serves also as the psalm's conclusion. This bracketing of the hymn with a call to give thanks not only indicates the nature of the psalm (a thanksgiving) but also suggests that it was originally used in a communal setting. Perhaps it was the occasion of an important individual's solemn entering of the Temple to express gratitude, perhaps a king returning successfully from battle. But of course on this day of the Lord's own making, we think of the King of kings who by his resurrection has triumphed over every evil force that threatens human happiness. We think and we give thanks, for we

know that Easter Sunday provides the clinching proof of the goodness of our God and of his endless loving mercy. In the psalm all 'the sons [and daughters] of Israel', the whole people, are invited to take up the cry: 'His love has no end.' Today, for even more powerful reasons than Israel's, we are called to give thanks for God's undying love.

'The Lord's right hand has triumphed; his right hand raised me up. I shall not die, I shall live and recount his deeds.'
In the second section of the psalm, the singer speaks of being caught up in a terrible plight and then of the way in which defeat was turned into victory. Only the strong 'right hand' of God, a symbol of his power, could have turned the catastrophe of Good Friday into the triumph of Easter Sunday; it was that hand that 'raised ... up' the crucified Christ. And, as St Paul says, 'Christ, being raised from the dead, will never die again; death no longer has dominion over him' (Romans 6:9). The risen Christ will never again face death; he lives for ever to 'recount [God's mighty] deeds'.

'The stone which the builders rejected has become the corner stone. This is the work of the Lord, a marvel in our eyes.'
And finally a wonderful word-picture highlights the incredible contrast between Jesus disowned and crucified, and Jesus ablaze with resurrection glory. On Good Friday he, God's chosen stone, had been 'rejected' by the 'builders' (the leaders of the people), who regarded him as surplus to their requirements. But on Easter Sunday it becomes clear that God has vindicated the rejected stone, making him 'the corner stone' or keystone of a new structure, the new people of God. It's fascinating to see how naturally this

metaphor of the discarded stone was used in the early Church in reference to Jesus' death and resurrection (Acts 4:11).

LET US PRAY: *Lord God, we are your Easter people; in the resurrection of your Son we 'have been brought back to true life'; and so we pray that, in the power of the Spirit, we may be renewed in mind and heart.*

Second Sunday of Easter

The rejoicing of Easter continues. Every Sunday is a 'little Easter', a celebration of the Lord's resurrection, but that is peculiarly so of the Sundays of Paschaltide.

In the first reading (Acts 5:12-16) Luke gives us a glimpse of the early Church. Its members are called 'the faithful'; what distinguished them from others is their belief in the risen Jesus. They witness to that belief by their lives and also by miracles, so that the number of believers continues to increase.

The second reading (Revelation 1:9-13,17-19) introduces a biblical book that has been called 'the gospel of the Risen Christ'; he is presented as 'the First and the Last', the one who was dead and now is alive for ever.

Today's gospel (John 20:19-31) recounts the events of the first Sunday after Easter Day. Thomas had been absent when the risen Lord appeared to the other disciples and gave them the resurrection gift of peace; but now, a week later, Thomas also is granted an appearance of the Lord. It elicits from him the magnificent confession: 'My Lord, and my God', and leads Jesus to assure us that the truly blessed ones are those (like ourselves) 'who have not seen and yet believe'.

Predictably, the responsorial psalm is again taken from Psalm 117. We have seen that originally it may have been associated with a king; we use it of *the* King, our risen Lord.

Prayerful Ponderings

'Give thanks to the Lord for he is good, for his love has no end.'
Today's response is taken from the opening words of the psalm.
However, there is an alternative: the psalmist's words may be
replaced by a triple 'Alleluia!' In either case the sense is much the
same: praise and glory and thanksgiving be to our God and to his
Son, risen from the dead, for their love which 'has no end'.

'Let the sons of Israel say: "His love has no end." Let the sons
of Aaron say: "His love has no end." Let those who fear the
Lord say: "His love has no end.'"
This opening litany calls upon all the people to acknowledge that
'his love has no end'. First, the invitation goes out to 'the sons [and
daughters] of Israel', the people in general; next to 'the sons of
Aaron', the priests; then to 'those who fear the Lord', possibly those
who believe in God though they do not belong to the Jewish
community; but, finally, on this day the invitation is addressed to us;
we too are encouraged to join in the chorus of grateful praise for
God's *hesed*, his ever-faithful love.

'The stone which the builders rejected has become the corner
stone. This is the work of the Lord, a marvel in our eyes. This
day was made by the Lord; we rejoice and are glad.'

Once more the reversal of fortune between Good Friday and Easter Sunday is vividly presented under the metaphor of a stone 'rejected' by the builders as of no consequence but later singled out as the all-important 'corner stone'. Significantly, Jesus himself had appealed to this very verse to indicate how the leaders of the people would cast him aside (Matthew 21:42). And once again there is the acknowledgement that this is 'a marvel' which only the Lord could have achieved. Hence, this day is of the Lord's own making or, as we simply say, it is the Lord's day: for us, as for Christians down through the ages, a day of rejoicing and gladness.

'O Lord, grant us salvation; O Lord, grant success.'
As we celebrate the glorious victory of the Lord, it is hardly surprising that we should beg him to 'grant us salvation', allow us to share in the fruits of his victory. Though the word 'success' appears nowhere in the New Testament, today it is fitting that we should take it upon our lips, for ultimately there is only one success that matters; it is that our lives are so centred upon the Lord, by faith and love, that we achieve the purpose for which he suffered, died and rose again, the purpose for which we were created.

'Blessed in the name of the Lord is he who comes. We bless you from the house of the Lord; the Lord God is our light.'
Originally this psalm may well have celebrated a royal victory. As the king made his solemn entry into the Temple, 'the house of the Lord', he was greeted with the joyous cry 'Blessed in the name of the Lord is he who comes'; and then the priests offered a blessing to the him and his cortege. On this day we cry out with joy as Christ our King, crucified and risen, enters the eternal 'house of

the Lord', his Father's house; 'we bless' him, in the sense of praising him, worshipping him, as our risen Lord; we thank him for being 'our light', the one who has brought meaning into our lives and the promise of salvation.

LET US PRAY: *Loving Father, we thank you for the gift of faith in your beloved Son and in his resurrection from the dead. May that faith, more precious than gold, be for us our strength, our joy and our salvation*

Third Sunday of Easter

The first reading of each Sunday until Pentecost is taken from the Acts of the Apostles, with its story of the infant Church, which was born out of the dying and rising of Christ. Today we hear how the apostles, despite threat of persecution, boldly announce that Jesus is risen (Acts 5:27-32, 40-41).

The second reading throughout Eastertide is taken from the Apocalypse (or book of Revelation). Its author tells of a vision in which he sees the whole of heaven's company united in worship of Christ, 'the Lamb that was sacrificed' (Revelation 5:11-14). In that worship we share.

Three times Peter had denied Christ during his passion; in today's gospel (John 21:1-19) we hear how he makes a threefold confession of his love for the risen Christ.

Psalm 29, from which today's responsorial psalm comes, is a glad song of praise and thanksgiving, particularly appropriate for the Easter season.

Prayerful Ponderings

'I will praise you, Lord, you have rescued me and have not let my enemies rejoice over me. O Lord, you have raised me from the dead, restored me to life from those who sink into the grave.'

During his days on earth Jesus often recited the psalms: they were his prayers. The early Christian writer Cassian imagines Jesus using today's psalm as he 'gives thanks to his Father after his glorious resurrection'. He praises the Father and thanks him because 'you have rescued me' from death; despite my apparent defeat on Good Friday, you 'have not let my enemies rejoice over me'. Why, 'you have [even] raised me from the dead', you have 'restored me to life', when there seemed to be no longer any hope for me.

'Sing psalms to the Lord, you who love him, give thanks to his holy name.'

We 'who love him' gladly 'sing psalms to the Lord' our God; we 'give thanks to his holy name' for all his mighty works and especially for the resurrection of his beloved Son. In the first reading we see the disciples rejoicing to suffer 'for the sake of the name' of the risen Jesus. The resurrection is at the heart of our faith and it is the pledge of our own resurrection from the dead. And so, with Jesus, we too can pray in the words of the psalm's refrain: 'I will praise you, Lord, you have rescued me' – even from the grave.

'His anger lasts but a moment; his favour through life. At night there are tears, but joy comes with dawn.'

Death, which the psalmist picturesquely attributes to God's 'anger', is only a temporary affliction, it 'lasts but a moment'; on the other hand, God's 'favour', his kindness to us, lasts 'through [eternal] life'. When the 'night' of death comes there may well be tears, but with the bright 'dawn' of resurrection they are replaced by a 'joy' that nothing can take away. Was it the realisation of this that gave the apostles such courage in the face of punishment and the threat of worse (see first reading)?

'The Lord listened and had pity. The Lord came to my help. For me you have changed my mourning into dancing; O Lord my God, I thank you for ever.'

These words might almost serve as a commentary on the event described in today's gospel. After his dreadful betrayal of the Lord on Good Friday, Peter was a broken man; how often he must have pleaded in his heart for forgiveness. Early in the morning, beside the Lake of Galilee, he was given a threefold opportunity to make amends for his betrayal. Three times over he proclaimed his love for Jesus ('Lord, you know that I love you'), and heard Jesus in reply entrusting to him his lambs and his sheep. In that moment Peter's 'mourning' was turned 'into dancing' and his great resolve was to praise and thank him 'for ever'.

LET US PRAY: *Father, as we celebrate with joy the glorious resurrection of your Son, Jesus, we pray that our whole life may be an 'Alleluia' of praise and gratitude to your name.*

Fourth Sunday
of Easter

The disciples begin preaching about Christ's death and resurrection in the synagogue at Antioch (present-day Turkey), but, meeting with rejection, they turn to the Gentiles. All nations are to hear the Good News (Acts 13:14, 43-52).

A huge throng from every tribe and nation gather before the 'throne of the Lamb'. Never again will they know hunger, thirst or tears (Revelation 7:9, 14-17).

In the gospel (John 10:27-30) Jesus speaks to us as the good shepherd, who expects us to listen to him, believe in him and follow him; and assures us that no one can ever take us away from him.

Psalm 99 is a perfect example of a hymn, a song of praise, and, with its reference to 'the sheep of his flock', an appropriate responsorial psalm for this Sunday.

Prayerful Ponderings

'Cry out with joy to the Lord, all the earth. Serve the Lord with gladness. Come before him, singing for joy.'

Eastertide is supremely the time for rejoicing. As the Easter Preface puts it: 'We praise you with greater joy than ever in this Easter season, when Christ became our paschal sacrifice.' And so today's psalm might be described as an Easter hymn: it bids us – and indeed 'all the earth' – to 'cry out with joy to the Lord', 'serve [him] with gladness' and come into his presence 'singing for joy'. It has been suggested that the words sound like a description of an audience with a king: you are to greet him with a cry of joy, to enter joyously into his presence, to promise to serve him faithfully. For the psalmist, it was an acknowledgement of the supreme Lordship of God; for us today it is also an acknowledgement that Jesus is Lord and that it is not merely our duty but our joy to come into his presence, to serve him, to be faithful to him.

'Know that he, the Lord, is God. He made us, we belong to him, we are his people, the sheep of his flock.'

The worship we offer is in itself a confession of faith; first, a confession that 'the Lord is God', that he and he alone is worthy of that title and of the veneration that goes with it; secondly, that 'he made us' and 'we belong to him', that we are his creation, not only because he made us and preserves us in being, but also because, through the death and resurrection of Jesus, he has transformed us into his sons and daughters; and thirdly that we are 'the sheep of his flock', called to listen to him, to follow him and to believe in him (see gospel).

'Indeed, how good is the Lord, eternal his merciful love. He is faithful from age to age.'

We praise the Lord because he is 'good', and if that sounds rather bland, the following words indicate why he is called good: because 'his merciful love', his covenant steadfastness, is never-ending, and is matched only by his faithfulness, his constancy, which lasts 'from age to age'.

LET US PRAY: *On this Easter day, Lord God, we rejoice that we are your people, the sheep of your flock, and we pray that we may always follow faithfully our Good Shepherd.*

Fifth Sunday of Easter

At the end of their missionary journey, Paul and Barnabas retrace their steps in order to encourage the Christian communities they have founded and to appoint 'elders' to take care of them (Acts 14:21-27).

A final vision from the Apocalypse (21:1-5) reveals 'a new heaven and a new earth' and God himself dwelling in the midst of 'his people'. This is the goal of all our striving.

In the gospel (John 13:31-35), Jesus teaches that it is by their love for each other that his followers are to be known during that period which extends from the first preaching of the gospel (first reading) to its final goal (second reading).

This Sunday's responsorial psalm, Psalm 144, sings of the glory of God's kingdom and of his all-embracing love.

Prayerful Ponderings

'I will bless your name for ever, O God my King.'

These words, which form the refrain for today's psalm, also set the tone for what follows. Prayers of blessing are very common in the Bible and here we have a prayer which blesses and praises God because, though so glorious, so transcendent ('O God my King'), he is also full of loving concern for all his creatures. The psalmist promises to bless his name 'for ever'; there's a sense in which today we are helping to fulfil that promise, as we take the psalmist's words upon our lips.

'The Lord is kind and full of compassion, slow to anger, abounding in love. How good is the Lord to all, compassionate to all his creatures.'

In this verse, which is perhaps a reflection of 'Israel's oldest theological assertion about God' (Brueggemann), it is fascinating to note that God is described not in those rather rarefied terms we commonly use – omniscient, omnipresent, unmoved-mover, etc. – but rather in the warm, down-to-earth, personal terms of kindness, 'compassion', slowness 'to anger', abundance of 'love'. Furthermore, this way of talking about God derives not from abstruse theological argumentation but from lived experience. Those who first sang these words had discovered for themselves the kindness, the compassion, the faithfulness of God; and we who have the wonderful good fortune of knowing Jesus Christ, the fullest possible revelation of God, must surely be ready to join our Jewish sisters and brothers in declaring: 'How good is the Lord to all, compassionate to all his creatures.'

'All your creatures shall thank you, O Lord, and your friends shall repeat their blessing.'
Just as God's goodness extends to 'all his creatures' so, in the psalmist's vision, the whole of creation is united in giving him thanks. Perhaps it would be better to say that while God's other creatures manifest his goodness, and to that extent 'thank' him for his goodness, simply by being what they are, it is only we human creatures who can be styled 'your friends' and only we who are able consciously to give him thanks.

'They shall speak of the glory of your reign and declare your might, O God, to make known to men your mighty deeds and the glorious splendour of your reign. Yours is an everlasting kingdom; your rule lasts from age to age.'
The first three Gospels leave us in no doubt that the kingdom of God was the principal theme of Jesus' teaching (see Mark 1:15 and parallels). This final verse of the psalm focuses on God's kingdom: unlike all earthly kingdoms, this is 'an everlasting kingdom', God's rule will never come to an end, for it 'lasts from age to age'. Meanwhile, we are exhorted to reveal to others 'the glory' and 'the splendour' of that 'reign', to 'declare' to others God's 'might', to 'make known' to others his 'mighty deeds'. There is no surer way of responding to this appeal than by ' the love [we] have for one another' (see gospel).

LET US PRAY: *O God our King, in this in-between time as we await the coming of your kingdom in its fullest glory may our lives be distinguished by a love that will lead others to acknowledge your reign and to experience your boundless goodness.*

Sixth Sunday of Easter

The first 'Council' of the Church meets in Jerusalem to decide a contentious issue of the day, how far converts from paganism must first embrace the practices of Judaism (Acts 15:1-2).

The heavenly Jerusalem, with the Lord God and the Lamb in its midst, fulfils all the hopes of Israel (Revelation 21:10-14, 22-23) and is the culmination of Christian history.

Jesus in the gospel (John 14:23-29) promises that he and the Father will dwell in those who keep his word, that the Holy Spirit will guide them and that they will enjoy the gift of peace.

Psalm 66 is a harvest song of thanksgiving. As the responsorial psalm of this Sunday, it serves on the one hand as a thanksgiving for the greatest of God's 'harvests' – the resurrection of Jesus and his sending of the Spirit – and on the other as a plea that all peoples may come to share in those blessings.

Prayerful Ponderings

'O God, be gracious and bless us and let your face shed its light upon us. So will your ways be known upon earth and all nations learn your saving help.'

In the book of Numbers (6:24-26) Moses is instructed by God to tell Aaron and his sons, the priests, how they are to bless the people and so assure them of God's continuing protective presence. There seems little doubt that the first verse of this psalm is a restatement of that blessing formula: it asks God to 'be gracious' to us, his people, to 'bless us' and let his 'face shed its light upon us'. However, the ultimate purpose is that 'all nations' may come to know 'your ways' and 'learn your saving help'. In this Easter season when we not only ask for God's blessing but celebrate the generous way he has already blessed us through the death and resurrection of his Son, this psalm might be read as a reminder that we have the duty of living out the events we celebrate in such a way that others may be brought to a knowledge of the Lord's saving ways.

'Let the nations be glad and exult for you rule the world with justice. With fairness you rule the peoples, you guide the nations on earth.'

God promised Abraham that he would be blessed and that through him and his descendants 'all the nations of the earth [would] gain blessing for themselves' (Genesis 22:17-18). It is in the spirit of that promise that our Jewish brothers and sisters have prayed this psalm over the centuries. And now we too take up the same appeal, begging that 'the nations' should learn about God and so be brought to 'exult' in him, to experience his 'justice' and 'fairness' and guidance. It is astonishing how a psalm which began as a thanksgiving for an earthly harvest of crops has become a prayer for a spiritual harvest of the whole world.

'Let the peoples praise you, O God; let all the peoples praise you. May God still give us his blessing till the ends of the earth revere him.'

As we consider today's readings, we can see that from the beginning (first reading) the Church's task has been to become truly catholic, reaching out to 'the ends of the earth' and including 'all the nations', and that its ultimate fulfilment will be achieved only in the heavenly Jerusalem (second reading) where 'all the peoples' are united in praise of God. In praying this psalm, it is good to recall that the blessings which we enjoy should lead to the salvation of men and women everywhere. With that thought in mind, we will gladly take upon our lips the daring refrain of today's psalm: 'Let the peoples praise you, O God; let all the peoples praise you.'

LET US PRAY: *Almighty God, on this day when we thank you for the glorious resurrection of your Son, we pray that by our lives we may help to hasten the day when every knee shall bow at the name of Jesus, the risen Lord.*

see page 263 for the feast of the Ascension

Seventh Sunday of Easter

Throughout its long history, the Church has never been without men and women who have laid down their lives for Christ; in today's first reading (Acts 7:55-60) we meet the first Christian martyr, Stephen, whose passion story closely resembles that of his Master.

Jesus, on the eve of his own passion, prays for all who will come to believe in him (ourselves included), that their unity may convince the world that he is sent by God (John 17:20-26).

Jesus, the Alpha and the Omega, promises that he will come soon, and the Spirit and the Bride (the Church) cry out: Maranatha – come, Lord Jesus (Revelation 22:12-14, 16-17, 20).

A few days ago we rejoiced in the Lord's ascension into heaven; today, using verses from Psalm 96, we rejoice in his exaltation as king of all the earth.

Prayerful Ponderings

'The Lord is king, most high above all the earth.'
This is one of a group of hymns known as the 'Enthronement Psalms' because they celebrate the enthronement of the Lord as king; according to some scholars, they formed part of a special annual liturgy in honour of his kingship. In any event the most common image of God in the Old Testament, and particularly in the psalms, is that of king; it is an image which exalts him and his reign, acknowledging that he is 'most high above all the earth'. It may have been the Exodus experience which first led Israel to think of Yahweh as a victorious king; for us in Paschaltide, it is especially the resurrection and ascension which leads us to praise our Lord as king.

'The Lord is king, let earth rejoice, the many coastlands be glad. His throne is justice and right.'
'The Lord is king' might simply be an assertion of Yahweh's ongoing reign: he is king and always has been. It might also be taken as an enthronement formula, a liturgical re-enactment of his coronation. Understood in the latter sense, it might be akin to the way in which we speak of the resurrection (or the nativity or any of the other great events of salvation history) as taking place today. The liturgy makes present the saving events of the past. And so as we celebrate the resurrection, we pray that all the 'earth' may

'rejoice' with us, that all 'the many coastlands' may share our joy. The fact that Jesus 'has taken his seat in heaven, on the right hand of that throne where God sits in majesty' (Hebrews 8:1), is itself an assurance that 'justice and right' will prevail.

'The skies proclaim his justice; all peoples see his glory. All you spirits, worship him.'
The whole universe is united in its acknowledgement of God's reign; 'the skies' above proclaim the 'justice' of that reign; 'all peoples' on earth have caught sight of 'his glory', the weightiness and wonder of his rule; and even the invisible 'spirits' are at one as they 'worship him'.

'For you indeed are the Lord, most high above all the earth, exalted far above all spirits.'
Today's readings, each in its own way, proclaim that the risen and ascended Jesus is 'indeed ... the Lord', 'the First and the Last, the Beginning and the End' (second reading); that he is 'most high above all the earth' and 'standing at God's right hand' (first reading); and that he is 'exalted far above all spirits', enjoying 'the glory you [the Father] have given [me] ... before the foundation of the world' (gospel).

LET US PRAY: *The Lord is risen and ascended into heaven, he is indeed King; and our prayer, heavenly Father, is that we may be renewed by the Spirit and so be made ready for that day when our King will come again.*

Pentecost

Today marks the end or, better, the climax of the Great Fifty Days of Eastertide: the coming of the Holy Spirit, and with it the birth of the Church, completes the redeeming work of Christ.

Today's gospel (John 14:15-16, 23-26) gives us Jesus' promise of the Holy Spirit under the title of 'Advocate' who will be with us for ever, calling to mind all that Jesus has taught. Jesus also pledges that whenever a person loves him and keeps his word, Father, Son and Holy Spirit will 'come to him and make [their] home with him'.

The first reading (Acts 2:1-11) retells the story of what happened on the first Pentecost day. The advent of the Spirit was like a new creation, the Church was born and the estrangement of the tower of Babel reversed as the disciples, now filled with the Spirit, discovered that what they said was understood by all their hearers, though they were of different races and different languages.

In the second reading (Romans 8:8-17) Paul declares that the Holy Spirit has 'made his home' in us; indeed, he says, 'unless you possessed the Spirit of Christ you would not belong to him'. It is because we are moved by the Spirit that we are children of God, able to call upon God as 'Abba' (dear Father); we are co-heirs of Christ, looking forward to heavenly glory.

The author of Psalm 103 – in today's Mass we have only a few excerpts from it – is not only a person of deep faith, one who sees that nature bears the fingerprints of its Maker and is kept in being by his Spirit, but also a poet who knows how to use language to celebrate what he sees. It reads like a poetical version of the creation account in Genesis 1.

Prayerful Ponderings

'**Bless the Lord, my soul! Lord God, how great you are! How many are your works, O Lord! The earth is full of your riches.**'
As you hear these words, you can almost imagine the poet standing beside the Creator as he gazes upon his work of creation and sees that it is good, very good. The psalmist gasps with wonder and delight: 'Lord God, how great you are!' The whole world seems to be alive with God's masterpieces. The poet bids his 'soul' bless the Lord, as though he wants his innermost deepest self to be involved in the wonder and the worship. On this day we are invited to share the psalmist's praise, remembering, however, that the Holy Spirit has worked a new and even more wonderful creation, in which we are enabled to call upon God as 'Abba' (dear Father).

'**You take back your spirit, they die, returning to the dust from which they came. You send forth your spirit, they are created; and you renew the face of the earth.**'
After reflecting on the countless creatures God had made, the psalmist marvels at the way he has provided for them all: their very 'spirit' (the Hebrew word also means 'breath') comes as gift from God; should he take it away, 'they die'; should he restore it again, 'they are created' and the whole of creation is renewed.

A slightly amended form of this verse, making it into a prayer that

God *will* send forth 'your Spirit [spelt with a capital "S"] and renew the face of the earth', is the refrain for today's responsorial psalm; we are surely meant to realise that if we give thanks to God for the gift of our life's breath, still more must we thank him that, through the gift of the Holy Spirit, he shares his own life with us: we are indeed renewed and transformed.

'May the glory of the Lord last for ever! May the Lord rejoice in his works!'
These words come from towards the end of the psalm. It is as though the psalmist is almost lost for words and can only say that he wants the Lord's 'glory' to go on and on for ever and at the same time wants the Lord to go on rejoicing in all 'his works'.

'May my thoughts be pleasing to him. I find my joy in the Lord.'
Finally, the plea that the psalmist's own 'thoughts', the psalmist's meditation, all that has been said in this psalm, may be like a 'pleasing' offering to the Lord. It is 'in the Lord' that the psalmist, and we too, find our best and lasting 'joy.'

LET US PRAY: *Creator God, you make all things new; come and, on this day of Pentecost, breathe your Holy Spirit into us anew so that we may work with you for the renewal of the whole world.*

The Most Holy Trinity

With the Easter season behind us, and just before returning to the Ordinary Sundays in the Year, we are invited by the Church to this celebration of the feast of the Most Holy Trinity.

In the first reading, from the book of Proverbs (8:22-31), divine Wisdom personified emanates from God, shares with him in his creative work and rejoices to 'be with the sons of men'. Is there a hint here of Jesus Christ, the Word made flesh?

We are 'at peace with God', St Paul declares (Romans 5:1-5), because of the gifts given us by the Son through the Holy Spirit, and are able to continue in faith and hope despite afflictions.

'Everything the Father has is mine' says Jesus (John 16:12-15), and all that Jesus has is given to us through the Spirit of truth.

Psalm 8 is one of the most magnificent songs of praise in the Psalter. Today, when we raise our voices in praise of the Blessed Trinity, verses from this song make up the responsorial psalm.

Prayerful Ponderings

'How great is your name, O Lord our God, through all the earth!'
The psalm is framed by this exclamation of praise, which appears at the beginning and the end of the song, and serves as the refrain of today's responsorial psalm. It is a cry of sheer delight at the greatness, the magnificence of 'your name'; 'all the earth' is filled with admiration of God's splendour. These words take on added significance for us to whom the mystery of the Trinity has been revealed; we rejoice in 'our God' and are filled with awe at the wonder of his being, he who is Three Persons in one God.

'When I see the heavens, the work of your hands, the moon and the stars which you arranged, what is man you should keep him in mind, mortal man that you care for him?'
Now comes the paradox; when I look up at the wonders of 'the heavens', when I see 'the moon and the stars which you arranged', I am struck by God's breathtaking greatness, but then when I look at 'mortal man [and woman]' in all their fragility and weakness, I am amazed that the Lord should give them a thought, that God should care for them at all.

'Yet you have made him little less than a god; with glory and honour you crowned him, gave him power over the works of your hand, put all things under his feet.'
Yet, the startling truth is that the Lord has made them 'little less than' gods. If these words seem incredible, they are no more so than

the words of today's second reading: 'the love of God has been poured into our hearts by the Holy Spirit'; we have been caught up into the life of the Trinity; we are the very sons and daughters of God. We do indeed have a royal dignity 'crowned' by the redeeming work of Christ 'with glory and honour'. In the words of Vatican II: 'In reality it is only in the mystery of the Word made flesh that the mystery of humanity becomes clear ... Christ ... in the very revelation of the mystery of the Father and of his love, fully reveals humanity to itself and brings to light its very high calling ... For by his incarnation, he, the Son of God, has in a certain way united himself with each individual' (*Gaudium et Spes* §22).

'All of them, sheep and cattle, yes, even the savage beasts, birds of the air, and fish that make their way through the waters.'
The previous verse spoke of the divine decree by which mere mortals have been given dominion over the whole of creation. This verse expounds that further. Clearly, weak mortal men and women have been greatly trusted: the mighty God himself has chosen in large measure to give us 'power over the work of [his] hand'. With that dignity comes also the responsibility to respect the whole of creation and to act as good stewards: without a practical concern for ecology it is difficult to see how we can give our God the praise which is the subject of this psalm from start to finish.

LET US PRAY: *Because we are so weak and yet are entrusted with so much, we pray that God the Father may encompass us, that God the Son may encircle us, and that God the Holy Spirit may enfold us with love now and for ever.*

see page 267 for the feast of the Body and Blood of Christ.

ORDINARY TIME

*Let
my prayer
rise
like incense
before
you*

ORDINARY TIME

'We thank thee that thy Church unsleeping,
while earth rolls onward into light,
through all the world her watch is keeping,
and rests not now by day or night.

'As o'er each continent and island
the dawn leads on another day,
the voice of prayer is never silent,
nor dies the strain of praise away.

'The sun that bids us rest is waking
our brethren 'neath the western sky,
and hour by hour fresh lips are making
thy wondrous doings heard on high.'

(John Ellerton 1826-1893)

Second Sunday in Ordinary Time

From the prophet comes the promise of universal rejoicing (Isaiah 62:1-5) as Jerusalem is restored and the people are addressed by God as his spouse, 'My Delight'.

In the gospel (John 2:1-11) there is rejoicing at 'the first of the signs given by Jesus': water turned into the rich new wine of the kingdom and Jesus revealing God's love for his people; it is significant that only a few chapters later John the Baptist refers to Jesus as 'the bridegroom' (John 3:29).

In the second reading (1 Corinthians 12:4-11) Paul speaks of the gift of the Spirit given to each for the good of all, an indication that God's kingdom has indeed come into this world.

Today's responsorial psalm, drawn from the verses of Psalm 95, catches the spirit of the other readings, for it is a song of joyful praise.

Prayerful Ponderings

'O sing a new song to the Lord, sing to the Lord all the earth.
O sing to the Lord, bless his name.'
We are called to take part in 'a new song to the Lord'. Each day
comes as a fresh creation from his hands and therefore each day, and
especially the Lord's day, demands that a new song of praise be
raised. The hope of the psalmist, which we must surely share, is that
the invitation to praise will be heard and answered in 'all the earth'
so that the men and women of all nations may 'sing to the Lord'
and 'bless his name'.

'Proclaim his help day by day, tell among the nations his glory and
his wonders among all the peoples.'
It is from this verse that the refrain of today's responsorial psalm comes,
a repeated call to 'proclaim the wonders of the Lord' and thereby give
him praise. For the psalmist the wonders include especially the
restoration of Zion/Jerusalem (first reading); for us they include the
mighty 'signs', such as the changing of water into wine (gospel), which
Jesus worked, thereby showing that God's kingdom is in our midst. A
practical aspect of our praise is to share the story of his wonders
'among all the peoples'.

'Give the Lord, you families of peoples, give the Lord glory
and power, give the Lord the glory of his name.'

The psalmist cannot resist the urge to summon all the 'families of peoples' to acknowledge 'the Lord', to give him 'glory and power', to recognise his universal sovereignty, the 'glory of his name' and his saving activity. Only when this is achieved will the Lord's purpose finally be fulfilled. Nor can we forget that the final words of Jesus were that we should take the good news to 'all nations'. At the heart of that good news is the fact that God loves us as a bridegroom loves his bride: through Jesus' life, death and resurrection we have become the 'Delight' of the Lord (see first reading).

'Worship the Lord in his temple. O earth, tremble before him. Proclaim to the nations: "God is king." He will judge the peoples in fairness.'
1 Chronicles 16:23f-42 recounts how the Ark of the Covenant, the sign of God's presence, was solemnly brought into 'his temple' at Jerusalem to the accompaniment of this psalm. Like other 'enthronement psalms', such as Psalms 46, 92, 94, 96, 97, this psalm may have been part of a liturgical service in which God's kingship was once more acknowledged; note the cry 'God is king', which is similar to the roar of welcome that greeted the coronation of an earthly king. However, this is a King of such awesome greatness that he is to 'judge the peoples', the kings included, and the very 'earth' is expected to 'tremble before him'.

LET US PRAY: *Almighty God and King, on this day we sing a new song of praise and thanks for your kingdom, revealed to us by your Son, Jesus; we rejoice that through him we have become your Delight, and we long for all peoples to find a place within your kingdom of love, to the glory of your name.*

Third Sunday in Ordinary Time

Today's first reading comes from the book of Nehemiah (8:2-6, 8-10), a lesser-known part of the Bible. It tells how, after the return from exile, the walls of the city were rebuilt; in today's passage, Ezra the priest addresses the assembled people, explaining God's Law and urging them to make 'the joy of the Lord' their stronghold.

The Law is also the theme of today's responsorial psalm. Psalm 18 is in two parts; the first section deals with the wonders of creation ('The heavens proclaim the glory of God') but the second, from which today's psalm comes, deals with the wonders of God's Law.

Today we are introduced to the Gospel that is to accompany us throughout the Sundays of this year, the Gospel of Luke, written in the 70s or 80s of the first century. We also listen to Jesus' inaugural address in which he announces that his coming is the fulfilment of the promises and the beginning of 'the Lord's year of favour' (Luke 1:1-4; 4:14-21).

Paul tells the incredible news that through baptism we have become members of one body, with Christ the head and we the members, each with our particular gifts and each dependent upon the others (1 Corinthians 12:12-30).

Prayerful Ponderings

'Your words are spirit, Lord, and they are life.'
Exceptionally, the refrain of the responsorial psalm is not to be found in the psalm of the day. Instead, it is borrowed from the sixth chapter of John's Gospel, where the disciples are shocked by our Lord's discourse on 'the bread of life', and he responds by assuring them that his spoken words are in all truth 'spirit and they are life'. The fact that this response is used in connection with Psalm 18 is another way of saying that Jesus' words are God's Law: they are not simply commands to be obeyed, but instruction to guide us on our journey through life.

'The law of the Lord is perfect, it revives the soul. The rule of the Lord is to be trusted, it gives wisdom to the simple.'
That 'the law' is referred to in so many different ways in this and the succeeding verses is itself an indication that it means something more than, for instance, the Ten Commandments. It refers to the revelation of God's will, which is to be found throughout the Bible, above all in the teaching of Jesus Christ, who is himself the Word of God and whose words are in all truth 'spirit and life'. This psalm is in the form of a litany of praises to God's Law, each word of praise having a similar structure: first, a characteristic of the Law is mentioned, and then a brief description is given of its beneficent effect. In this verse it is spoken of as 'perfect', flawless, and as 'the rule ... to be trusted', and its

effects are to revive 'the soul' (which means that it puts new spirit into our whole being), and to give us 'wisdom'

'The precepts of the Lord are right, they gladden the heart. The command of the Lord is clear, it gives light to the eyes.'
The description of the Law continues: God's Law is now spoken of in terms of 'precepts' which 'are right' and a 'command' which is 'clear'; and we are assured that it both gladdens 'the heart', our innermost self, and gives 'light to the eyes', so that we are no longer walking in the darkness of ignorance or unbelief.

'The fear of the Lord is holy, abiding for ever. The decrees of the Lord are truth and all of them just.'
Respect for the Law leads to a reverential 'fear' which is itself 'holy' and has repercussions that abide 'for ever'. And the Lord's 'decrees', again not to be thought of simply in terms of rules and regulations but rather in terms of the total guidance given us by his word, are 'truth', utterly reliable; and of course they are 'just' and righteous.

'May the spoken words of my mouth, the thoughts of my heart, win favour in your sight, O Lord, my rescuer, my rock!'
The psalm ends with a prayer, a request from the psalmist that 'the spoken words of my mouth', presumably a reference to this psalm, and 'the thoughts of my heart', from which it arose, may 'win favour in your sight'. However, it ought also to be the prayer of all who take the psalm on their lips; though the words may be the words of another, yet I want to make them mine so that they well up from my heart, and then, I trust, they will indeed 'win favour' with the Lord who is 'my rescuer' and 'my rock'.

LET US PRAY: *Grant, almighty God, that we may develop such a loving and living devotion to holy Scripture that your words, which are spirit and life, may be for us both a stronghold and a source of joy.*

Fourth Sunday in Ordinary Time

Jeremiah, having been chosen by God, is confident that despite trials and tribulations God will never fail him (Jeremiah 1:4-5, 17-19).

In the gospel (Luke 4:21-30) Jesus, like Jeremiah, meets with fierce hostility. On this occasion he walks unharmed through the midst of his opponents; it will not always be so.

In Psalm 70, against a background if not of persecution at least of trial and distress, the psalmist sings of confident trust in God who has never failed him.

St Paul's wonderful hymn to love (1 Corinthians 12:31-13:13) insists that there is no genuine value in anything, not even in handing over one's body to be burned, unless it is motivated by love.

Prayerful Ponderings

'In you, O Lord, I take refuge; let me never be put to shame. In your justice rescue me, free me; pay heed to me and save me.'
From the outset, the psalmist's position is made clear by the prayer: 'In you, O Lord, I take refuge'. In the psalms, to take refuge in the Lord or to make the Lord one's refuge is a way of expressing complete trust in the Lord, especially in times of trial or affliction (see first reading and gospel). As we shall see, this is the psalm of an elderly person. Having had a lifetime's experience of being helped by the Lord, the psalmist has no hesitation in praying 'never [to] be put to shame' or pleading in a variety of ways – 'rescue me', 'free me', 'pay heed to me', 'save me' – that there may be a happy outcome to present trials.

'Be a rock where I can take refuge, a mighty stronghold to save me; for you are my rock, my stronghold. Free me from the hand of the wicked.'
There is no way of knowing what precisely is meant by 'the hand of the wicked'; but possibly it is a metaphorical reference to the usual problems of old age, such as declining powers, as well as the distress caused when younger people ('the wicked') mock their elders, forgetting that one day they too will be old. In any event the psalmist's repeated petitions for help are matched by repeated cries of confidence: God is my 'refuge', my 'mighty stronghold', 'my

rock'. Indeed, the note of confidence is struck so often and so urgently that some scholars wonder whether this psalm should not be classified as a psalm of confidence rather than a psalm of petition; in other words, pleas for help seem to be almost incidental to expressions of confidence.

'It is you, O Lord, who are my hope, my trust, O Lord, since my youth. On you I have leaned from my birth, from my mother's womb you have been my help.'

Once more the psalmist makes a profession of complete confidence: 'You, O Lord, are my hope'; all life through, ever 'since my youth', you have been 'my trust'. It's 'on you I have leaned' since I was a tiny child. Indeed, truth to tell, you were 'my help' since the days when I was still in 'my mother's womb'.

'My lips will tell of your justice and day by day of your help. O God, you have taught me from my youth and I proclaim your wonders still.'

There is no mention of love in this psalm (see second reading); yet one is left with the unmistakable impression that this elderly person is deeply in love with the Lord in whom such absolute trust is placed. That, surely, is why it is asserted that the psalmist's 'lips' will 'day by day' and for ever be used to 'tell of your justice' and to 'proclaim your wonders'. The reference to 'my youth' hints that that time is now far off; in other verses, unfortunately not included in today's responsorial psalm, it is stated clearly: 'Do not reject me now that I am old' and 'Now that I am old and grey-headed, do not forsake me, God.' In all truth, this is an ideal psalm for all who are not as young as they used to be!

LET US PRAY: *We pray, Lord of all times and seasons, that as the years go by our confidence in you will never falter and that in old age, and even when death draws near, we shall still be proclaiming your unfailing goodness.*

Fifth Sunday
in Ordinary Time

In the *debir,* the most sacred part of the Temple, Isaiah is granted a vision of God's heavenly court. There, seraphim proclaim God's holiness and, after initial hesitation, Isaiah volunteers to be God's messenger (Isaiah 6:1-8).

Just as the Temple vision overwhelmed Isaiah with a sense of unworthiness but then led him to become God's messenger, so the miraculous catch of fish first filled Peter with a sense of unworthiness, but then prepared him and his companions to follow Christ's call and become his disciples (Luke 5:1-11).

Paul too (1 Corinthians 15:1-11), called to bear witness to the resurrection, is keenly aware of his unworthiness to proclaim Christ's message but finds courage in 'the grace of God that is with me'.

Finally, the responsorial psalm, Psalm 137, is a song of gratitude and praise in which the singer marvels at God's greatness, displayed especially in his readiness to stoop down to his insignificant creature.

Prayerful Ponderings

'I thank you, Lord, with all my heart, you have heard the words of my mouth. Before the angels I will bless you. I will adore before your holy temple.'

The psalm begins with a prayer of heartfelt thanks to the 'Lord' who 'heard the words of my mouth'. In earlier times, when every nation claimed to have its god, Israel regarded these national deities as altogether inferior to the God of Israel, but when it finally realised that he was the one and only God, the so-called gods came to be regarded as at best angels in the court of Yahweh (see first reading). So the psalmist wishes to 'bless' God in the presence of the 'angels', his heavenly courtiers – we cannot forget that at every Eucharist it is 'with all the choirs of angels in heaven [that] we proclaim your glory' – and he wishes to 'adore' God in his 'holy temple', the place of his special presence.

'I thank you for your faithfulness and love which excel all we ever knew of you. On the day I called, you answered; you increased the strength of my soul.'

Though the psalm is presented in the form of an individual's prayer, it is possibly meant to serve as a prayer for the whole community of Israel who have experienced a 'faithfulness and love' at God's hands which far excelled their expectations. The members of the Christian community can certainly make this prayer their own, thanking God for showing us a kindness and steadfastness beyond anything we could have imagined, answering our prayers, helping us in our weakness. Like Isaiah, Peter and Paul, we have discovered that, despite our unworthiness, the Lord is ready to increase our 'strength' and use us for his purposes.

'All earth's kings shall thank you when they hear the words of your mouth. They shall sing of the Lord's ways: "How great is the glory of the Lord!"'

With the psalmist we too should desire the coming of that day when 'all earth's kings' (that is to say, all the peoples of the world, since a king was regularly regarded as standing for his people) will hear of 'the Lord's ways', will join us in giving thanks and, having caught a glimpse of his 'glory' and magnificence, will gladly sing: 'How great is ... the Lord'. Of course that day will not come unless those who have heard the Good News share it with others, and so become true disciples of the Lord, like Peter and his companions (see the gospel). It is worth noting how frequently the vision of the psalmists is universal in scope: it is not confined to Israel but takes in the whole world. Is there not a challenge in that for us?

'You stretch out your hand and save me, your hand will do all things for me. Your love, O Lord, is eternal, discard not the work of your hand.'

The psalm ends with renewed acknowledgement of the way in which 'you stretch out your hand and save me' and the confident statement that 'your hand will [continue to] do all things for me', in the sense that you will continue the good work you have begun. We may be insignificant creatures in the immensity of the universe and yet God's steadfast 'love' for us has no end, it 'is eternal' and because we are 'the work of your hand' there will never come a time when God will 'discard' us.

LET US PRAY: *Hear our prayer, O Lord our God; in the presence of the mighty angels we praise you and we thank you, and we place all our trust in you, because we know that we are the work of your hands and you will never cast us aside.*

Sixth Sunday in Ordinary Time

Humankind has always been haunted by the quest for happiness. Jeremiah, the prophet, teaches us that a choice has to be made: either we trust in human beings or we trust in God. The first will lead to a dead-end wilderness, the second to true and lasting happiness (Jeremiah 17:5-8).

Psalm 1, the responsorial psalm for today, makes much the same point as Jeremiah and in part uses similar imagery. It is not by accident that this psalm features at the beginning of the Psalter: it seems certain that (together with Psalm 2) it was added after the rest of the collection was completed as a way of inviting us to recognise that the whole of the Psalter is a book of instruction, a pathway to happiness.

The psalm begins with a beatitude: 'Happy indeed is the man...' and the gospel (Luke 6:17, 20-26) gives us St Luke's version of our Lord's Beatitudes: 'How happy are those...'

In the second reading (1 Corinthians 15:12, 16-20) Paul points to the resurrection as the source of our hopes, and so of our happiness: if Christ had not risen we should be of all people the most unfortunate; but he has risen and so we are the most blessed.

Prayerful Ponderings

'Happy the man who has placed his trust in the Lord.'
The refrain does not come from today's psalm, as we might expect, but from Psalm 39. It begins, as does Psalm 1, with a beatitude ('Happy the one who ...') and broadly speaking sums up the teaching of Psalm 1: there is happiness for the person 'who has placed [his or her] trust in the Lord'. However, unlike Psalm 1, it begins on a positive rather than a negative note. Indeed, it may well have been selected as the response to the psalm in order to give a positive ring to the responsorial psalm as a whole.

'Happy indeed is the man who follows not the counsel of the wicked; nor lingers in the way of sinners nor sits in the company of scorners.'
This is a 'wisdom' psalm, not so much a prayer as a meditation, a reflection on how true happiness is to be found. It begins by briefly indicating the kind of person who will not find it: the one 'who follows ... the counsel of the wicked', or the one who 'lingers in the way of sinners', or the one who 'sits in the company of scorners'. There seems to be an intentional gradation, as though the psalmist were saying: It's bad enough to follow the ways of the wicked, but even worse to linger with them, and worst of all to sit in their company, to make yourself at home with them, above all when they are not simply 'sinners', wrongdoers in general, but 'scorners', those who ridicule the ways of God.

'... but whose delight is the law of the Lord and who ponders his law day and night.'

Now comes the positive aspect of the psalm: 'Happy indeed' is the one 'whose delight is the law of the Lord'. The law, Torah, is primarily divine instruction, rather than rules and stipulations; it includes all that tradition has taught about the ways and the will of the Lord. Understood in that sense, the law is something to 'delight' in, something to mull over 'day and night'. At the heart of all spirituality is the unwavering search to know and follow God's will. The basic theme of this psalm is close to that of the first answer in the 'penny' Catechism, wellknown to many older Catholics: 'God made me to know him, love him and serve him in this world, and be happy with him for ever in the next.'

'He is like a tree that is planted beside the flowing waters, that yields its fruit in due season and whose leaves shall never fade; and all that he does shall prosper.'

Now the psalmist presents the lesson of the previous verses in picture form; the one 'whose delight is the law of the Lord' is like a fine upstanding 'tree', a luxuriant tree which 'yields its fruit in due season', an evergreen 'whose leaves ... never fade'. Such a person, says the psalmist, 'shall prosper'. The comparison to a fruitful tree serves to remind us that just as a good crop of fruit is the natural outcome of a tree's being 'planted beside ... flowing waters' (see first reading), so the final outcome for those who love the law is not so much a form of reward for good behaviour but rather a natural fruitfulness which comes of their being united with the Lord of life and his will.

'Not so are the wicked, not so! For they like winnowed chaff shall be driven away by the wind.'

On the other hand there are 'the wicked' and theirs is a very different fate: their apparent success is all an illusion. They are like the lightweight 'chaff' at harvest time, for when the farmer throws his corn into the air, the heavy grains fall to the ground and are later collected, but the chaff is so insubstantial – simply an empty husk – that it is simply whisked away 'by the wind': what an ignominious end!

'For the Lord guards the way of the just but the way of the wicked leads to doom.'

Finally, a one-liner which summarises the psalm as a whole: a choice has to be made, for there are two pathways through life. The one, 'the way of the just', is guarded by 'the Lord' and so, by implication, is full of promise for those who walk in it; the other, 'the way of the wicked' has no lasting future: it 'leads to doom'. Experience would perhaps make us hesitate about describing life in such black-and-white terms, with no shades of grey in between. However, it is worth noting that the notion of the two ways runs through the Bible, and in the end a choice has to be made: are we people who build our house on rock or on sand (Matthew 7:24-27), are we to be numbered with the sheep or the goats (Matthew 25:33)?

LET US PRAY: *Lord, life is indeed more complex than this psalm seems to suggest, but let us not forget that a choice has to be made, that upon it depends our hope of eternal happiness and that the small choices we make each day are fashioning our fundamental option on which everything depends.*

Seventh Sunday in Ordinary Time

David, the future king of Israel, shows immense magnanimity in sparing the life of his persecutor, King Saul, though it is doubtful whether the latter would have done the same for David had the roles been reversed (1 Samuel 26:2, 7-9, 12-13, 22-23).

The episode of the first reading prepares us for today's gospel, where we hear Jesus exhorting us to show forgiveness even to our enemies, to 'be compassionate as your Father is compassionate' (Luke 6:27-38).

St Paul teaches us (1 Corinthians 15:45-49) that though there is much of the 'earthly Adam' in us all, yet our ambition must be to live and love after the example of the 'heavenly Adam', Jesus Christ.

The responsorial psalm, taken from Psalm 102, is a glorious song of praise and gratitude for the Lord's own compassion and love.

Prayerful Ponderings

'My soul, give thanks to the Lord, all my being, bless his holy name. My soul, give thanks to the Lord and never forget all his blessings.'

Throughout the three-year cycle of Sunday Masses, there is no psalm which appears more often than Psalm 102. Nor is that surprising, for it expresses in powerful fashion a sense of bewildered gratitude towards our God, in particular for that attribute of his which through all the ages, from the time of the psalmist to the present day, has always meant so much to sinful men and women, namely, his divine compassion. We ought to find little difficulty, therefore, in following the psalmist's example and bidding our whole selves ('my soul' and 'all my being') to 'give thanks to the Lord' for his goodness, to 'bless his holy name' in gratitude and 'never [to] forget' the multitude of 'blessings' we have received.

'It is he who forgives all your guilt, who heals every one of your ills, who redeems your life from the grave, who crowns you with love and compassion.'

Some of the most wonderful of those blessings are now spelt out: forgiveness of 'all [our] guilt', healing of all our 'ills', protection of our 'life' from death and 'the grave', and the crowning of our lives 'with [his] love and compassion'. However, God's greatest blessing of all is his Son, Jesus, and in the light of that blessing the psalmist's list takes on an altogether more wonderful significance for not only does God forgive all our sins and heal the damage they leave in their wake, he also 'redeems [us] from the grave' (not of course by saving us from death but by delivering us out of death) and, in his 'love and compassion' he 'crowns' us with royal dignity as his own sons and daughters, destined to live with him for ever.

'The Lord is compassion and love, slow to anger and rich in mercy. He does not treat us according to our sins nor repay us according to our faults.'

'The Lord is compassion and love' is the refrain of today's psalm. It also marks the start of Israel's most ancient creed, an expression of their fundamental belief about 'the Lord'. Seldom if ever in the Old Testament do we meet a description of God which so closely approaches that of John's brief yet dazzling assertion: 'God is love' (1 John 4:8). It tells us that 'God is compassion', where the Hebrew word (*rahum*) suggests a mother-like tenderness; that his 'love' is such that on the one hand he is 'slow to anger', and on the other he is 'rich in mercy'. He is the utterly dependable One, and so 'he does not treat us' as we deserve, he does not pay us back 'according to our faults'.

'As far as the east is from the west so far does he remove our sins. As a father has compassion on his sons, the Lord has pity on those who fear him.'

Instead, he tosses away 'our sins' as far as they can go, 'as far as the east is from the west'. The 'compassion' he shows is not only mother-like (see previous verse) but also like that of 'a father' for 'his sons' and daughters. There is a particular poignancy in these words on a day when Jesus makes it clear (gospel) that we are expected at least to strive to imitate the endless compassion of the most perfect father, 'your Father in heaven': we are to love enemies, to do good to those who hate us, to do to others as we would have them do to us. God has loved us and forgiven us, we are expected to do the same for others.

LET US PRAY: *God our Father, on this day your Son sets us a task that seems completely beyond us, to be compassionate even as you are compassionate; we beg you, God of the impossible, to enable us to approach the high ideal of forgiveness which Jesus presented not only by his words but also by his deeds.*

Eighth Sunday in Ordinary Time

Sirach, the author of Ecclesiasticus, from which today's first reading comes (17:24-29), suggests that just as a sieve is proved by the flour it produces, or a kiln by the pot it fires, or a tree by the fruit on its branches, so our worth – or lack of it – is proved by our speech.

Like Sirach, Jesus uses everyday images in his teaching; having warned against the danger of judging others, he states that just as a tree's value is judged by its fruits so the true test of human virtue is the way we live our lives (Luke 6:39-45).

St Paul looks towards the day of judgement, encouraging his hearers to persevere in doing good in the assurance that working for the Lord can never be working in vain (1 Corinthians 15:54-58).

The verses selected from Psalm 91 as the responsorial psalm for this Sunday speak of the value of continual gratitude to God but also paint a picture of the sturdiness of the man or woman of virtue.

Prayerful Ponderings

'It is good to give thanks to the Lord, to make music to your name, O Most High, to proclaim your love in the morning and your truth in the watches of the night.'

It could hardly be expressed more simply or more clearly. Without any word of explanation, as if to imply that this goes without saying, there is the plain statement that 'It is good to give thanks to the Lord'. Thanksgiving is pleasing to him, a way in which we can 'make music' to the 'Most High'. Ultimately all thanksgiving whenever it is made, whether 'in the morning' or 'in the watches of the night', is a proclamation of his 'love' and of his faithfulness; and, particularly in the context of today's readings, of the love and faithfulness he shows towards those who are just.

'The just will flourish like the palm-tree and grow like a Lebanon cedar.'

There's an obvious change of topic at this point; in fact, several of the intervening verses, which tell how the just find their delight in the wonderful works of God, have been omitted – and now the psalm focuses upon 'the just' themselves. (The Hebrew word for 'the just' is in the singular referring to an individual but since 'they' appears in the next verse it is perhaps more convenient to use the plural throughout.) In their uprightness and their ability to survive the most frightful storms and still 'flourish', they are compared to 'the palm-tree'; while in their nobility and grandeur, they are compared to the most magnificent of all the Mediterranean trees, a mighty 'Lebanon cedar'.

'Planted in the house of the Lord, they will flourish in the courts of our God, still bearing fruit when they are old, still full of sap, still green, to proclaim that the Lord is just.'

The natural nobility of the trees just referred to is further enhanced, and the trees themselves afforded additional protection, when they are 'planted' in the precincts of the Temple 'of the Lord', where they would never be vandalised. And the just are like them: it's not that they enjoy eternal youth (a very dubious boon!) but rather that even 'when they are old' they still go on 'bearing fruit', and are always keenly aware of where their fruitfulness comes from, always ready 'to proclaim that the Lord is just'. It is surely the hope of us all that even in old age we shall, spiritually speaking, 'still [be] full of sap, still green'.

'In him, my rock, there is no wrong.'

We have seen above how 'the just' is initially used in the singular (the just man or woman); now, in this final verse, the singular form is found once again. Perhaps it was originally intended to be the word of the leader of the community, speaking on behalf of all the people. In any event on this Sunday each of us is invited to make it his or her own: we acknowledge that the Lord is 'my rock' and 'there is no wrong' in him.

LET US PRAY: *Lord, loving and faithful, we give you thanks for enabling us to bear good fruit and we pray that to the end of our days we may continue to flourish and be fruitful.*

Ninth Sunday in Ordinary Time

In a true ecumenical spirit, King Solomon prays that God will respond not only to Jews but also to non-Jews who come to pray in the Temple, the building that symbolises the heart of Jewish faith (1 Kings 8:41-43).

In the gospel (Luke 7:1-10) the foreign centurion realised that Jesus, a devout Jew, would be rendered unclean by entering his house, yet he had faith enough to believe that Jesus, who had come for all, could still reach out and cure his sick servant.

Faced with Judaisers, who maintained that observance of the Jewish law was necessary for salvation, Paul solemnly affirms that there is only one Good News and it is for all, no matter what their nationality (Galatians 1:1-2, 6-10).

Psalm 116 has the distinction of being the shortest of all the 150 psalms. Though just two verses long, it is universal in its outlook.

Prayerful Ponderings

'Go out to the whole world and proclaim the Good News.'
This, the refrain for today's responsorial psalm, does not of course
come from the psalm itself but rather from the final section of
Mark's Gospel, where the risen Christ bids his disciples take the
message of the gospel 'to the whole world', to 'proclaim the Good
News' everywhere and to everyone.

**'O praise the Lord, all you nations, acclaim him all you
peoples!'**
It could be taken for granted that the praise of God is the special
concern of the People of God. One of the extraordinary features
of this psalm, and others like it, is that it longs for that praise to arise
from 'all you nations', so that 'all you peoples' will 'acclaim him'.
The implication seems to be that the praise of God is incomplete,
is lacking something vital until and unless the whole world is
involved in the faith and the joy of speaking God's praises. There is,
and can be, only one God and his worship cannot be hemmed in
by national boundaries nor can the songs of praise be restricted to
any individual language.

'Strong is his love for us; he is faithful for ever.'
It has often been noted that Psalm 116 is a perfect example of a
'psalm of praise'. It begins (see previous verse) with a call to praise

which, in this case, is addressed to the universal family of humankind. That invitation is then followed (see this verse) by a reason, or reasons, for the praise. One might have expected that the universality of the call would have been rooted in the fact of creation (all are creatures of the one God), but – another extraordinary feature of this psalm – in fact it is based upon the saving work of God. His love (*hesed*) and his faithfulness (*emet*) undergird his covenant relationship with his people Israel, established after he had rescued them from slavery. However, Israel is meant to be a bridgehead whereby that relationship may be extended to all the world.

As Christians, we have been given still greater proofs of just how 'strong is his love' and how 'faithful' is his steadfastness. Through the saving work of Christ all the men and women of all the nations, of all times and all places, have been redeemed, all have been made, in principle at least, into the sons and daughters of God. If ever there was a psalm for the Lord's day, this is surely it; but if we pray it, we must also be prepared to bear witness through our lives to the love and faithfulness of God revealed through Jesus Christ our Lord.

LET US PRAY: *Lord of all creation, may Jesus, the faithful One and the true, possess our hearts always, and may our lives, however humble, help to lead all nations and all peoples to praise you.*

Tenth Sunday
in Ordinary Time

Elijah revives the dead child of the widow who offered him the hospitality of her home (1 Kings 17:17-24).

The gospel is an obvious parallel to the first reading for it tells how Jesus, moved with compassion for the widow of Nain, raises her dead son to life. Raising the dead to life was one of the great signs associated with the Messiah: 'everyone was filled with awe' (Luke 7:11-17).

Today's psalm consists of verses from Psalm 29 which offer praise and thanks to God for having come to the rescue of the psalmist when apparently on the point of death.

In the second reading (Galatians 1:11-19) Paul speaks of the wonderful transformation by which he, a persecutor of Christians, became an apostle of Christ, a preacher of the Good News.

Prayerful Ponderings

'I will praise you, Lord, you have rescued me and have not let my enemies rejoice over me.'

The responsorial psalm's refrain, which coincides with the first half of this verse, is at once a declaration of the purpose of the psalm: to praise and thank God ('I will praise you, Lord'); and of the reason for the praise/thanksgiving: to acknowledge the deliverance accomplished by the Lord ('you have rescued me'). In those far-off days, just as today, there were always people who seemed to take pleasure in the misfortunes of others; and so the verse goes on to say that the psalmist's 'enemies', whoever they may have been, will no longer have any reason to 'rejoice' over the misfortunes.

'O Lord, you have raised my soul from the dead, restored me to life from those who sink into the grave.'

It seems that the psalmist's misfortune was some dreadful illness which almost proved fatal: he had almost joined 'those who sink into the grave'; in fact the psalm reads very much like the prayer prayed by King Hezekiah, when he felt close to death (Isaiah 38). In any event, the Lord intervened: he came to the rescue, he 'restored me to life'. And so there is an outpouring of rejoicing and gratitude, just as there was, in today's readings, on the part of Elijah and 'the mistress of the house' and the widow of Nain – not to mention the two sons, rescued from the grave! Nor ought we to forget that Jesus constantly expressed gratitude: he was always ready to thank his Father for favours received. It was because he was such a grateful man that he was so hurt by the ingratitude of others, such as the lepers he had cured and who failed to return to give thanks (Luke 17:11-19).

'Sing psalms to the Lord, you who love him, give thanks to his holy name.'

In the gospel 'everyone was filled with awe' at the extraordinary action of Jesus, and praise of him and his reputation 'spread all through the countryside'. This verse is an invitation to the faithful everywhere to join the psalmist and continue to 'give thanks' to God for his favours. However, we can use the opportunity afforded by this psalm to express our gratitude for all God's favours, not least those which we have experienced personally. 'Sing psalms to the Lord, you who love him' should serve as an encouragement to all who use the psalms in their prayer: it is an indication, the psalmist seems to say, that they are to be numbered among those 'who love [the Lord]'.

'His anger lasts a moment; his favour through life. At night there are tears, but joy comes with dawn.'

Once God is acknowledged as Creator of all that is, it is tempting – it's a temptation to which the psalmist seems to have succumbed – to make him responsible for all that happens, the bad as well as the good. It is a short step from that to attribute the trials of life to 'his anger' and the good things to 'his favour'. Christian theology might not be too happy with such a presentation of God; nonetheless, there is a lesson for us in the way that the psalmist recognises, as we sometimes fail to do, that the bad times, in general, last but 'a moment' while the good times last 'through life'; or, to put it another way, 'the tears' are like overnight guests, but 'with the dawn' comes 'joy'. If only we 'count our blessings', we are likely to find that blessings – such as the basic blessing of life itself – far outweigh the misfortunes.

'The Lord listened and had pity. The Lord came to my help. For me you have changed my mourning into dancing.'
Towards the end of the psalm – some of the intermediate verses have been omitted – the psalmist once again tells the story of a wonderful deliverance, how 'the Lord listened and had pity', how he 'came to my help', turning 'mourning into dancing'. St Paul's own conversion (see second reading) might have been described in similar terms – from mourning into dancing.

'O Lord my God, I will thank you for ever.'
The psalmist's final words are in the form of a promise to 'thank you for ever'. We too are meant to follow that example: when brought before God in prayer, so many of the experiences of our lives, in particular transformations of bad times into good, become occasions for unceasing praise and thanksgiving. And without doubt our eternal destiny will be to 'thank [God] for ever'.

LET US PRAY: *Lord God, our greatest Benefactor, we praise and thank you for giving us the blessing of life together with the promise of eternal life to come; may we remain always grateful to you until that day when all our mourning is finally transformed into eternal dancing in our Father's house.*

Eleventh Sunday
in Ordinary Time

Nathan the prophet's fearless denunciation of David for adultery and murder leads the king to repentance (2 Samuel 12:7-10, 13).

The woman 'who had a bad name in the town' receives forgiveness for the faith and love she shows in bathing Jesus' feet with her tears, kissing them and anointing them (Luke 7:36 – 8:3).

St Paul, who had himself been transformed from persecutor into preacher of Christ, declares that his life now consists in faith in Jesus 'who loved me and who sacrificed himself for me' (Galatians 2:16, 19-21).

Psalm 31 is a song of joy sung by a sinner whose sins have been forgiven. It is from this psalm that today's responsorial psalm is taken.

Prayerful Ponderings

'Forgive, Lord, the guilt of my sin.'

This refrain is not strictly speaking an excerpt from Psalm 31 but it does serve as an excellent summary of one of the salient points of the psalm, namely, that sins must be acknowledged if they are to be forgiven. Each of today's readings offers an example of the wonderful reward which awaits sinners who recognise their sinfulness and seek forgiveness.

'Happy the man whose offence is forgiven, whose sin is remitted. O happy the man to whom the Lord imputes no guilt, in whose spirit is no guile.'

The psalm proper begins with a beatitude for the 'forgiven' sinner, adopting a formula similar to that used by Jesus in the Sermon on the Mount: O 'happy', truly blessed, is 'the man [or woman] whose sin is remitted', the one, therefore, 'to whom the Lord imputes no guilt' for the simple reason that no guilt now remains: there has been a complete pardon. How fortunate, we might add, to have a God so generous with forgiveness wherever true repentance is found!

'But now I have acknowledged my sins: my guilt I did not hide. I said: "I will confess my offence to the Lord." And you, Lord, have forgiven the guilt of my sin.'

The psalmist's own experience underlies these words, though they might easily be the words of the repentant David, or the converted Paul, or the forgiven woman of ill-repute in the gospel. More important still, these are words which we, the followers of Christ in the twenty-first century, can make our own. Sin is as old as the human race and as new as the latest piece of news to slip off the press. Time and time again men and women have discovered that acknowledgement of sin, a refusal to hide guilt, a readiness to confess have brought great peace.

'You are my hiding place, O Lord; you save me from distress. You surround me with cries of deliverance.'

The verses immediately preceding this one – unfortunately they are not included in today's responsorial psalm – describe how difficult life had been, how difficult sleep had been too, so long as the psalmist carried about the burden of guilt unacknowledged; and it even began to affect his health. Because we have all experienced the relief of forgiveness it is not difficult for us to make the psalmist's sentiments our own: God became our 'hiding place' where we could own our sins and seek forgiveness, and then we were relieved of our 'distress'; like captives who'd been set free, we felt as though we wanted to shout aloud our 'cries of deliverance'.

'Rejoice, rejoice in the Lord, exult, you just! O come, ring out your joy, all you upright of heart.'

The psalmist rejoices, every repentant sinner rejoices, and we too 'rejoice in the Lord' and 'exult'. We want others to become 'upright of heart' by seeking God's forgiveness so that they also can 'ring out their joy'. It's said that St Augustine, the sinner who became a saint, had this psalm affixed to the wall above his bed so that it would be one of the first things he would see on waking each morning. For him thanksgiving for sins forgiven was a permanent feature of life.

LET US PRAY: *In a world where sin is widely unacknowledged, where it is often treated as a kind of superstition, we beg you, loving Lord who gave yourself up on the cross for our sins, not to allow us to adopt such attitudes; may we always be ready to own up to our guilt so that we may experience the joy and release that come from your forgiveness.*

Twelfth Sunday in Ordinary Time

Speaking prophetically of the Messiah to come, Zechariah (12:10-11; 13:1) declares that the people will one day 'look on him whom they have pierced' and 'mourn for him as for an only son'.

In the gospel, when Jesus has been acknowledged by Peter as the Messiah, he at once declares that he is destined to suffer and die – he is to be the pierced one – and that his followers must in their turn be prepared to take up the cross (Luke 9:18-24).

St Paul teaches us that at baptism we have clothed ourselves in Christ: there is no escaping the responsibilities of those made one with the suffering Messiah (Galatians 3:26-29).

Psalm 62, with its burning words about longing and thirsting for God, is many people's favourite prayer, and today it is our responsorial psalm.

Prayerful Ponderings

'O God, you are my God, for you I long; for you my soul is thirsting. My body pines for you like a dry, weary land without water.'

There is an unmistakable note of fervour in the psalmist's voice; this is a person who prays, who is able to speak of God as 'my God', who knows what it is to 'long' for him, to have a 'soul' that is 'thirsting' for him, and a 'body [that] pines' for him like a piece of 'dry, weary land', crying out for the rain. We may not be able to match the impassioned words of the psalmist, yet we too have a deep-down yearning for the Lord; that's why we keep on striving to be faithful to our prayers day after day. And that is also why we can happily use the words that make up today's refrain: 'For you my soul is thirsting, O God, my God.'

'So I gaze on you in the sanctuary to see your strength and your glory. For your love is better than life, my lips will speak your praise.'

It was 'in the sanctuary' that the psalmist sought an answer to that longing and yearning for God that he felt so keenly; there, it was possible to become aware once more of God's 'strength' and of God's 'glory'. And so the psalmist makes a wonderful declaration – that 'your love is better than life [itself]' – and a firm resolve – that 'my lips will [not cease to] speak your praise'. As men and women who have been clothed in Christ, we are called to be prayerful people. We seek the Lord in 'the sanctuary', in that place – the local church, perhaps, or a corner of the bedroom at home, or the area in front of an icon – which is special to us, our sanctuary, because it is the place where we normally speak to God in prayer, where we are constantly assured of his nearness, of the strength and glory of his presence, where we at least move towards a recognition that nothing in life is to be preferred to his love for us, and where we determine to be resolute in raising our voice to him in praise.

'So I will bless you all my life, in your name I will lift up my hands. My soul shall be filled as with a banquet, my mouth shall praise you with joy.'
The psalmist again voices a resolve to 'bless [God] all my life', to 'lift up my hands' in prayer day by day, convinced that this will be as satisfying as sharing in 'a banquet' and that the opening of 'my mouth' in 'praise' will always be a 'joy'. Again we may feel that we cannot compete with the eloquence of the psalmist: so often for us prayer seems to be demanding rather than rewarding. Nonetheless there are also times when we appreciate what the psalmist is trying to express: times when prayer is sweet, more deeply satisfying to our inmost self than any banquet could ever be; in our heart of hearts we know that our hearts cannot find rest except in him (St Augustine). And even on more difficult days, the fact that we continue to 'lift up [our] hands' in prayer is itself a proof that we believe that time spent with the Lord, however inadequately, is never time wasted.

'For you have been my help; in the shadow of your wings I rejoice. My soul clings to you; your right hand holds me fast.' Today's psalm is rounded off with this splendid act of both confidence and resolve which we are invited to make our own. First confidence, which is based on past experience, the undeniable fact that in so many of the difficulties of life 'you have been my help', you have been like a mother hen protecting me under 'the shadow of your wings'. Then resolve to persevere, especially in prayer. It's a perseverance which has two faces: on the one hand 'my soul clings to you' – there is my side of the venture; on the other hand, even when I seem to be clinging only with my finger tips, 'you right hand holds me fast' – there is God's side of the venture. Following the advice of St Ignatius, let us pray as though all depends upon us, but with the conviction that in the end all depends upon him.

LET US PRAY: *As we think of Jesus, pierced for our sake, faithful to your love even to death, we are led to pray, holy Father, that we may persevere in our following of him, not least in his prayerfulness throughout all the ups and downs of life.*

Thirteenth Sunday in Ordinary Time

In response to the call to follow Elijah as prophet of Israel, Elisha leaves his own people and sacrifices all his possessions (1 Kings 19:16, 19-21).

As he sets out on his final journey to Jerusalem, Jesus makes it clear that his followers must abandon any apparent sources of security, and be prepared to put the claims of the kingdom first, without any looking back (Luke 9:51-62).

In today's beautiful song of confidence, taken from Psalm 15, the psalmist rejoices in having the Lord as 'my portion and cup'.

Paul reminds us that the liberty to which Christ calls us is inextricably linked with that love which finds its vital source in the Holy Spirit (Galatians 5:1, 13-18).

Prayerful Ponderings

'Preserve me, God, I take refuge in you. I say to the Lord: "You are my God."'

The psalm begins with a brief petition for God's protection. The motive for that request is that 'I take refuge in you', a standard formula in the psalms for entrusting one's self to the Lord's care, especially in time of danger. A sign of that complete trust is to be found in the fact that the psalmist is able to declare quite simply, 'You are my God', with the further implication, 'I belong to you, I am yours.'

'O Lord, it is you who are my portion and cup; it is you yourself who are my prize.'

The expressions describing God as 'my portion and cup' and as 'my prize' are not simply expressions of rejoicing at the close links that exist between the psalmist and God; they are also part of the vocabulary used in the book of Joshua where it tells how the Promised Land was divided out among the people of Israel. After God had first led his people out of slavery into freedom and then to the conquest of Palestine, each tribe and clan received its own particular God-given portion. The psalmist, therefore, is saying: 'My portion is more valuable than a piece of territory; I have you yourself, Lord, as my share, and I desire nothing more.' Such an attitude springs from single-mindedness which is one of the themes running through today's readings: Elisha, Paul and above all Jesus himself show in their lives that God is all that they desire, their prize above all else.

'I will bless the Lord who gives me counsel, who even at night directs my heart. I keep the Lord ever in my sight: since he is at my right hand, I shall stand firm.'

The remainder of the psalm is a song of joyful trust in the Lord who keeps the psalmist ever in his care, 'even at night' providing 'counsel' and directing the 'heart'. And in response the singer of this song promises to 'bless the Lord' and to 'keep the Lord ever in my sight'. The mere thought that the Lord is 'at my right hand' means that 'I shall stand firm', I shall not be moved, I shall be safe.

'And so my heart rejoices, my soul is glad; even my body shall rest in safety. For you will not leave my soul among the dead, nor let your beloved know decay.'

'Heart', 'soul' and 'body' are caught up in celebration of God's protective care; the whole person 'rejoices', 'is glad', is able to 'rest in safety'. So lively is the faith, so complete the commitment of the psalmist that it seems inconceivable that the union with God would ever be brought to an end, even by death. 'The hope, though vague as yet, is leading towards a belief in eternal life', says a footnote to this verse in the Jerusalem Bible. Indeed, the first Christians appealed to this very psalm as proof of our Lord's resurrection: it was, they argued, inconceivable that God would leave his Son 'among the dead' or 'let [his] beloved know decay' (Acts 2:25-32).

'You will show me the path of life, the fullness of joy in your presence, at your right hand happiness for ever.'

The praying of Psalm 15 is an ideal way of renewing our baptismal commitment to follow Jesus faithfully. Because we are united with him, the final sentence of the previous verse has its significance for us: though our bodies will one day 'know decay', we shall not be left for ever 'among the dead'. On the contrary, as this verse suggests, God has opened for us 'the path of [eternal] life', has given us the promise of 'fullness of joy in [his] presence', has assured us of 'happiness for ever' at his 'right hand'.

LET US PRAY: *On this day, Lord our God, we reaffirm our determination to be wholehearted in our following of Jesus Christ your Son, and as he was raised from the dead so may we too rise to eternal life, to the fullness of joy and happiness at your right hand.*

Fourteenth Sunday
in Ordinary Time

Today's first reading (Isiah 66:10-14) is a summons to Israel to rejoice in the restoration of Jerusalem; once thought to be as good as dead, she is now like a mother giving birth to God's children and bringing them comfort.

The gospel (Luke 10:1-12, 17-20) also speaks of rejoicing, the rejoicing of the 72 disciples at the end of their first mission. However, Jesus points to an even better reason for rejoicing: 'that your names are written in heaven'.

Though Paul does not use the word joy (Galatians 6:14-18), he does speak of his 'only boast', the cross of Jesus Christ through which salvation has been won and joy brought into the whole world.

The note of joy reverberates in today's responsorial psalm, taken from the hymn, Psalm 65.

Prayerful Ponderings

'Cry out with joy to God, all the earth, O sing to the glory of his name. O render him glorious praise.'

Predictably, today's refrain is the opening words of the psalm, for they re-echo the rejoicing to be found in the other readings today. 'All the earth' is exhorted to join in the celebration, to 'cry out with joy to God', to 'sing to the glory of his name', to 'render him glorious praise'.

'Say to God: "How tremendous your deeds! Before you all the earth shall bow; shall sing to you, sing to your name!"'

The reason for the universal rejoicing is the awesome nature of what God has done; the whole earth is invited to say to him, 'How tremendous your deeds!' and to acknowledge that he is deserving of the worship of peoples everywhere; they should 'bow' before him and 'sing to your name'.

'Come and see the works of God, tremendous his deeds among men. He turned the sea into dry land, they passed through the river dry-shod. Let our joy then be in him; he rules for ever by his might.'

Now the nature of God's 'tremendous ... deeds' is briefly sketched: 'he turned the sea into dry land, they [the people] passed through the river dry-shod'. The reference is obviously to the Exodus, the foundational event in Israel's history. However, that is not all. The Hebrew words for 'sea' (*yam*) and 'river' (*nahar*) were also the names of the chaotic powers which, according to an ancient myth, were defeated by Baal, the Canaanite god of wind and storm. The implication is that Israel's God is far superior to Lord Yam and Lord Nahar – not to mention His Excellency Baal, the storm god – he is sovereign Lord of all the earth. At the Exodus the people sang a song of rejoicing, and now the congregation – the psalm was part of a temple service – are to follow that example, singing out 'our joy' that our God 'rules for ever by his might' over gods and nations alike. In some sense the Exodus event is made present in and through their worship, which is why the nations are invited to 'come and see'. How much greater should be our rejoicing at the re-presentation of the saving death and resurrection of Jesus at every Mass.

'Come and hear, all who fear God. I will tell what he did for my soul. Blessed be God who did not reject my prayer nor withhold his love from me.'

At this point an individual, perhaps the temple priest, summons the congregation, 'all who fear God', to 'come and hear' the story of his own experience. He leaves us with little more than two basic facts, one of them expressed rather negatively: first, he called on God, and, second, God 'did not reject my prayer nor withhold his love from me'; and yet those two facts speak of a relationship with God which is full of trust, on the part of the petitioner (otherwise, why pray at all?), but also based on the goodness of our God, who never rejects our prayers and never withholds his love.

LET US PRAY: *God of Calvary and of the empty tomb, we rejoice in you and bow down before you, who, through the dying and rising of your Son Jesus Christ, have displayed your tremendous deeds and assured us of your unchanging love.*

Fifteenth Sunday
in Ordinary Time

Through the covenant, says Moses, God is close to his people; they must keep his commandments, which have already been made known to them (Deuteronomy 30:10-14).

Jesus, in the gospel, indicates that love of God and of neighbour constitute the greatest commandment of all; however, the 'neighbour', as the parable of the Good Samaritan shows, is not simply a fellow believer but whoever is in need (Luke 10:25-37).

The letter to the Colossians (1:15-20) begins with a magnificent prologue which shows that, through 'his death on the cross', Jesus is revealed as the Good Samaritan, the one who brings salvation to all the world.

In the psalm for today, taken from Psalm 68, a person in distress calls upon the Lord for help, confident of his compassion.

Prayerful Ponderings

'This is my prayer to you, my prayer for your favour. In your great love, answer me, O God, with your help that never fails.'
As so often in prayers of petition ('laments', as they are often called), the theme of confidence runs through this psalm from beginning to end; and so, having declared 'this is my prayer ... for your favour', the psalmist immediately speaks of confidence, confidence in the 'great love' of God, confidence in his 'help that never fails'. It is as though the psalmist had caught a first glimpse of the Lord's boundless compassion which will one day lead him to take upon himself the role of Good Samaritan for all the nations (see gospel).

'Lord, answer, for your love is kind; in your compassion, turn towards me.'
Continuing the thought of the previous verse, the psalmist begs the Lord to 'answer', to 'turn towards me' and once again confidently acknowledges that his 'love is kind', that he is a God of 'compassion'.

'As for me in my poverty and pain let your help, O God, lift me up. I will praise God's name with a song; I will glorify him with thanksgiving.'
The psalmist knows what it means to endure 'poverty and pain'.

The cause of the suffering is unknown to us, even though it is spoken of at great length, especially in the earlier part of the psalm (which does not form part of today's responsorial psalm); indeed, the psalm begins with the cry 'Save me, O God, for the waters have risen to my neck' – like the cry of a drowning person! Clearly the pain was intense and even then the sufferer met with derision and insults from opponents. It has been noted that no other psalm has been used so extensively in the New Testament by way of allusions to Christ and particularly to his sufferings. We might use it, therefore, as a helpful reflection on the One who in the time of his passion bore mockery and scorn for our sakes (second reading). Moreover, the note of praise ('I will praise God') and gratitude ('I will glorify him with thanksgiving,) might serve as a reminder that beyond the passion lies the glory of resurrection.

'The poor when they see it will be glad and God-seeking hearts will revive; for the Lord listens to the needy and does not spurn his servants in their chains.'
If, as the psalm asserts, the sufferer's salvation is going to serve as a source of encouragement to others, especially 'the poor' and all 'God-seeking hearts', then how much more the salvation won for us 'by his death on the Cross' and the glory of his resurrection. Today's refrain, 'Seek the Lord, you who are poor, and your hearts will revive', is based on this verse.

'For God will bring help to Zion and rebuild the cities of Judah. The sons of his servants shall inherit it; those who love his name shall dwell there.'
This verse, like the preceding one, is concerned not so much with

an individual but with the whole nation. For example, the mention of 'his servants in their chains' may well be a reference to those who are suffering in exile; similarly the requests for 'help to Zion' and the rebuilding of 'the cities of Judah' seem to speak of a time when the whole nation is facing the aftermath of some disaster. Possibly these verses were added at a later date so that a psalm originally intended for one person, might now be extended in its meaning to cover the whole nation. The people of Israel were ready to re-apply a psalm, sometimes with slight variations or additions, to a current situation; we can do the same and make today's psalm a prayer for all those members of the People of God who are facing persecution in various parts of the world.

LET US PRAY: *In the spirit of this psalm, we pray, Lord, with confidence that all who suffer, especially those who suffer for conscience's sake, may experience the loving compassion of the Good Samaritan who made peace for us all by his death on the cross.*

Sixteenth Sunday
in Ordinary Time

The first reading (Genesis 18:1-10) presents a delightful picture of Bedouin hospitality: Abraham recognises the presence of God in the three strangers whom he welcomes.

The story of Martha and Mary (Luke 10:38-42) suggests that, where hospitality is concerned, being busy about many things is not as important as being present to one's guest.

Psalm 14, today's responsorial psalm, is an 'entrance liturgy', one which raises the question: who is a fitting guest in God's house?

Paul, imprisoned for the faith, is confident that by sharing in the sufferings of Christ he can enrich the Church (Colossians 1:24-28).

Prayerful Ponderings

'Lord, who shall dwell on your holy mountain?'

The opening words of the psalm are in the form of a question. It is asked by would-be worshippers who are about to enter the Temple on that 'mountain' (Zion) which is 'holy' because the Lord has designated it as his particular dwelling place in the midst of his people. In fact Psalm 14 actually begins with the words – omitted, unfortunately, in today's responsorial psalm – 'who shall be admitted to your tent?', which come immediately before 'dwell on your holy mountain'. The 'tent' was the family home for nomadic people; it was their territory, others were admitted only as guests. To come into God's tent, to 'dwell' with the Almighty, therefore, was to be his guest, and it behoved guests to enquire what the 'Lord' himself might require of them, for he is a holy God.

'He who walks without fault; he who acts with justice and speaks the truth from his heart.'

The response is not simply in terms of ritual observances but rather of a person's inner integrity; such a person 'walks without fault' because that integrity is reflected in daily behaviour, and especially in relationships with others. Some of the implications – the list is not meant to be exhaustive – are 'justice' in what people do, and 'truth' in what they say. 'He who walks without fault' is almost a technical description of the 'just' or holy person in Israel; and so the refrain 'The just will live in the presence of the Lord' becomes a summary of the whole psalm.

'He who does not slander with his tongue. He who does no wrong to his brother, who casts no slur on his neighbour, who holds the godless in disdain, but honours those who fear the Lord.'

The ideal expressed in the previous verse is now expanded, in particular the necessity of 'truth from the heart' in one's dealings with others. It precludes 'slander', 'wrong to [one's] brother [or sister]', and 'slur on [one's] neighbour'. It involves honouring 'those who fear the Lord'. We might be reluctant to add, as the psalmist does: 'and hold[ing] the godless in disdain' but that seems to be the poet's unsophisticated way of saying that the just person must take his or her stand, on the side either of the godless or of the God-fearers. There can be nothing in between.

'He who keeps his pledge, come what may; who takes no interest on a loan and accepts no bribes against the innocent.'

Thoughts turn now to the wider society. Its well-being depends, as the just person knows, upon the keeping of a 'pledge, come what may', accepting 'no bribes against the innocent' and taking 'no interest on a loan'. (In a society, unlike our own, where people never borrowed except in direst need, exacting interest was tantamount to taking advantage of a fellow human being's distress; and so was condemned.)

187

'Such a man will stand firm for ever.'

Entrance liturgies begin with a question about what is required of those who wish to worship the Lord, followed by a list of the requirements; finally, a blessing is pronounced, perhaps by a temple priest. In this psalm the blessing is a promise that the person who behaves in the way outlined in the psalm will not only be admitted into God's presence but 'will stand firm for ever', his or her whole life will be enriched. The lesson to be drawn from this psalm is not that we may worship God only if we have lived up to the highest ideals but rather that if we worship him (if we are allowed to 'dwell in his tent') then our aim and ambition should be to reflect something of his holiness in our daily living.

LET US PRAY: *We give you thanks, God our Father, that you welcome us into your house despite all our sins and shortcomings and there offer us such generous hospitality; we pray that by the way we live our lives, and especially the way we treat others, we may bear witness to your great holiness.*

Seventeenth Sunday in Ordinary Time

Abraham (Genesis 18:20-32) is shown bargaining with God in an attempt to save the doomed cities of Sodom and Gomorrah.

While at Sodom there were not even ten just men, whose presence would have saved the city, through one Just Man, Jesus Christ, forgiveness has been won for the whole human race (Colossians 2:12-14).

In the 'Our Father' Jesus gives us the model Christian prayer and assures us that, through the Spirit, gift of the Father, we are God's children; in his parable of the man who continued to knock at his neighbour's door, he teaches us the importance of persistence in prayer (Luke 11:1-13).

Psalm 137, which provides us with today's responsorial psalm, is a song of thanksgiving for God's generous response to the psalmist's prayer.

Prayerful Ponderings

'I thank you, Lord, with all my heart, you have heard the words of my mouth.'

In the light of the Lord's readiness to respond to Abraham's appeal (first reading) – albeit after a certain amount of haggling! – and Jesus' own promise that prayers will always be heard and the Father will always offer good gifts, even the Holy Spirit, to those who approach him, today's psalm could hardly be more appropriate. It begins with a simple statement of the psalmist's intent, which is to 'thank you, Lord'. Nor is the thanks simply a matter of form: it is wholehearted, given 'with all my heart'. And the reason for such gratitude? The psalmist's prayer has been answered: 'you have heard the words of my mouth'.

'Before the angels I will bless you. I will adore before your holy temple.'

We do not know the nature of the difficulties which led the psalmist to appeal for God's help, but, whatever they were, thanks are to be given publicly; stationed perhaps in the forecourt of the Temple, the psalmist now bows in worship towards 'your holy temple'; it is there that the Lord is believed to dwell, surrounded by his court of angels. It is possible that 'angels' (*'elohim*) should be translated 'gods', in which case the pagan gods are referred to: in reality they are non-gods, serving merely as courtiers in the house of the Lord God of Israel.

'I thank you for your faithfulness and love which excel all we ever knew of you. On the day I called, you answered; you increased the strength of my soul. The Lord is high yet he looks on the lowly and the haughty he knows from afar.'

The psalmist now points out that while 'faithfulness' and 'love' are characteristic of the God who entered into covenant with his people, on this occasion they have been experienced by the singer of the psalm to an incredible degree, excelling 'all we ever knew of you'. The fact is that 'on the day I called', you responded by bringing me deliverance; you 'increased the strength of my soul'. Unlike the 'gods' of the nations, 'the Lord' shows that he is truly God because, though 'high', he draws close and attends to 'the lowly' people, while keeping his distance from those who are 'haughty' and self-sufficient.

'Though I walk in the midst of affliction you give me life and frustrate my foes. You stretch out your hand and save me, your hand will do all things for me.'

It is the unique character of the true God, displayed in his concern for the lowly, that leads the psalmist to trust him even – perhaps, especially – 'in the midst of affliction'; for his strong right 'hand' is always ready to 'give life', to 'save', to 'frustrate my foes', whoever or whatever they may be. We who have heard Jesus' promise (gospel) that all prayer is heard by our great God who is also 'our Father' ought to be outstanding for our gratitude to God: 'No duty is more urgent', St Ambrose used to say, 'than that of giving thanks.'

'Your love, O Lord, is eternal, discard not the work of your hands.'

A final confession of trust: the covenant 'love' and faithfulness of God is unchanging, 'is eternal'. That is why we can so confidently beg him not to ignore the lowly and the poor for they too are 'the work of your hand.'

LET US PRAY: *Give us, good Lord, a heart always sensitive to the many gifts you have bestowed on us and always filled with gratitude that you hear so readily the prayers of your sons and daughters, the beloved work of your hands.*

Eighteenth Sunday in Ordinary Time

The author of Ecclesiastes, or to give it its Hebrew name Qoheleth (= the Preacher), strikes a pessimistic note, as he queries whether life has any meaning: work, wealth, worry – all seem to be vanity (Ecclesiastes 1:2; 2:21-23).

In striking contrast to the first reading, the letter to the Colossians (3:1-5, 9-11) shows how certainty of the resurrection puts everything into a new perspective: our 'life is hidden with Christ in God' and our supreme task is to fix our eyes on the risen Lord.

Jesus confirms the lesson of the second reading, for he warns that hoarding riches is hardly worth the work and worry it costs; all that really matters is making oneself rich in God's sight (Luke 12:13-21).

The responsorial psalm, taken from Psalm 94, urges us to 'listen to [the Lord's] voice today', where 'today' means the present moment.

Prayerful Ponderings

'Come, ring out our joy to the Lord; hail the rock who saves us. Let us come before him, giving thanks, with songs let us hail the Lord.'

This is one of a cluster of psalms which salutes God as King. A procession wends its way up the slope that leads to the Temple. As the pilgrims 'come before [the Lord]', they sing a hymn expressing the spirit in which they approach the holy presence – it would be good to think that we come to Sunday worship with similar enthusiasm – it is a spirit of joy in the Lord ('Come, ring out our joy to the Lord') and a spirit of gratitude for his saving work ('hail the rock who saves us'). The people of Israel regarded salvation not simply as an event of the past but, through their participation in the liturgy, as a present reality. The reminder that God is their rock of salvation may well have led them to gaze across at the huge rock on which the Temple was built and rejoice that, because of the Lord's saving work, they are even more firmly grounded than is the house of the Lord.

'Come in; let us bow and bend low; let us kneel before the God who made us for he is our God and we the people who belong to his pasture, the flock that is led by his hand.'

As they make their way into the sacred precincts, the pilgrims seem to be urging one another on: 'let us bow', they say, let us 'bend low', 'let us kneel'. Bowing, bending low, kneeling – before this great God it is right that one should perform such actions, should make oneself small and so acknowledge even with the body that he is 'the God who made us', or, to follow a more accurate translation, the God who is making us: creation, like salvation, is both something already achieved and also an ongoing process. Moreover, as the psalm now says, 'he is our God'; therefore, we belong to him, we are his possession. To proclaim that we 'belong to his pasture', that we are his 'flock ... led by his hand' is more than resorting to a pastoral metaphor: in ancient times it was common to speak of a king as shepherd of his people; and so in this psalm we acknowledge that the Lord is our King and that we are in his safekeeping.

'O that today you would listen to his voice! "Harden not your hearts at Meribah, as on that day at Massah in the desert when your fathers put me to the test; when they tried me, though they saw my works."'

On a day when the readings powerfully remind us that life has lost its true meaning unless we seek 'the things that are above', and when we have just accepted that the Lord is our Shepherd King, it is hardly surprising that we should be urged to 'listen to his voice'. The quotation marks suggest that at this point another voice (that of God, perhaps, through a temple prophet?) warns that even God's people can fail, as they did 'at Meribah' (=dispute) and 'at Massah' (=testing), where they disputed with the Lord, even 'put [him] to the test' (see Exodus 17:7). In the early Church this psalm, and especially this verse, was used to warn Christians of the danger of falling away 'from the living God' (see Hebrews 3:7-19); the warning is no less necessary today. Little wonder that this verse, or at any rate its opening, forms the refrain to today's responsorial psalm: if we are to 'make ourselves rich with God', it is vital that our attitude be that of the young Samuel: 'Speak, Lord, for your servant is listening' (1 Samuel 3:9).

LET US PRAY: *Because you are our Shepherd King, we beg you, Lord, to help us to set our hearts upon you, to listen willingly to your voice and to follow you fearlessly and lovingly, so that to the end of our days we may never fall away from you.*

(Exceptionally, there is an alternative responsorial psalm for today, Psalm 89:3-6, 12-14, 17; see below, Twenty-Third Sunday in Ordinary Time.)

Nineteenth Sunday in Ordinary Time

It was during the night, the book of Wisdom recalls (18:6-9), that the Exodus from Egypt to the Promised Land began.

In the gospel Jesus teaches that while the kingdom has in one sense already come, in another it is still to come, and so it is vital that we be ready to meet the Master whenever he returns, even if it be in the middle of the night (Luke 12:32-48).

The second reading is a hymn to the men and women of faith, the virtue which alone can steel us to keep watching and waiting for the Lord's arrival (Hebrews 11:1-2, 8-19).

Verses from Psalm 32 paint an encouraging picture of those who are chosen by the Lord and who in their turn place their trust in him. These verses serve as today's responsorial psalm.

Prayerful Ponderings

'Ring out your joy to the Lord, O you just; for praise is fitting for loyal hearts.'

As in so many of the psalms known as hymns, this one speaks both of 'praise' and 'joy'; it seems to hint that where there is the one, true praise, there also is the other, an overflowing joy (in fact the Hebrew word suggests loud shouts of joy!). The *Catechism of the Catholic Church* describes praise as 'the form of prayer which recognizes most immediately that God is God. It lauds God for his own sake and gives him glory ... It shares in the blessed happiness of the pure of heart' (§2639). Since in a sense praise of God is doing what comes naturally to a human being, it might be argued that that is why it brings happiness with it. At any rate the psalm is clear: both praise and joy are to be expected of those who are 'just', of those who are right with the Lord, of those who may be described as 'loyal hearts', where God is concerned.

'They are happy, whose God is the Lord, the people he has chosen as his own.'

Again reference is made to the happiness of those 'whose God is the Lord', but immediately we are reminded that that is so because he, not they, took the initiative; they are 'his people' because 'he has chosen [them] as his own'. The people of Israel believed that in their history was being worked out God's plan for the whole human race. As Christians, we too are his chosen people, a thought which ought to give us a deep sense of happiness and the realisation that through the Church the Lord himself is continuing his saving work. We should have no difficulty in making the refrain of the psalm our own: 'Happy are the people the Lord has chosen as his own.'

'The Lord looks on those who revere him, on those who hope in his love, to rescue their souls from death, to keep them alive in famine.'

From happiness the psalm turns to hope. It tells us that 'those who revere [the Lord]', who hold him in reverential awe, who place all their 'hope in his [boundless] love' can be assured that he 'looks on' them. And when the Lord looks upon people, he does so with compassion, he does so in order to help and sustain them, 'to rescue' them from dangers and 'to keep them alive in famine'. Of course this does not have to be taken simplistically, as though we are to be saved miraculously from all adversity, that if, for example, we live in famine-stricken areas of the world, we are to be delivered from that situation, without more ado. The promise is rather that if we place our hope in the Lord then whatever happens, even if it be a famine, we shall not meet with any lasting (or, more accurately, any everlasting) harm.

'Our soul is waiting for the Lord. The Lord is our help and our shield. May your love be upon us, O Lord, as we place all our hope in you.'

The psalm draws to a close with a prayer that is first of all an assertion that we are 'waiting for the Lord' (see today's gospel and the second reading): we wait for him because we believe that he 'is our help [in all our needs] and our shield [against all that threatens our well-being]'. Secondly, our prayer is a plea that his faithful 'love' may always rest 'upon us'. And finally it is a simple yet powerful statement of complete trust in him: 'we place all our hope in you'.

LET US PRAY: *It is our joy to praise you, Lord our God, and to express our trust in you. As we await the day of your coming in a spirit of hope and of confidence so may your love rest upon us all the days of our life.*

Twentieth Sunday in Ordinary Time

Jeremiah had the unenviable task of telling his compatriots to trust in God rather than political alliances (38:4-6, 8-10) – not a very popular theme at the best of times. In the persecution he suffers for speaking out fearlessly, he is a figure of Christ himself.

In the gospel Jesus reveals his human anxiety at the prospect of facing a fiery ordeal and the 'baptism' of death; but he will be faithful to his task and urges his followers to do likewise, and, when need be, to make costly decisions, including those which involve our nearest and dearest (Luke 12:49-53).

The letter to the Hebrews (12:1-4) brings words of encouragement for those who face hostility because of their following of Christ: they are able to draw strength from Christ's own example who 'endured the cross' but is now 'at the right of God's throne'.

A selection of verses from Psalm 39 makes up today's responsorial psalm; it speaks of the way in which God came to the aid of the psalmist – as he came to Jeremiah's aid and above all to the aid of his Son, Jesus.

Prayerful Ponderings

'I waited, I waited for the Lord and he stooped down to me; he heard my cry.'

The psalmist begins his song by looking to the past and recalling the wonderful way in which God rescued him. There was the long, long wait, and during that time many prayers, but in the end 'he heard my cry' and 'stooped down to me'. The latter expression is the psalmist's way of saying that God had compassion on him, but, as we shall see in the next line, it was an altogether practical compassion; it involved God's coming to his rescue, either directly or through the intervention of someone else.

'He drew me from the deadly pit, from the miry clay. He set my feet upon a rock and made my footsteps firm.'

In the very words that Jeremiah himself might have used when he was hauled out of the muddy, waterless pit, by Ebed-melech the court official, the psalmist now describes how 'he' – the rescue is attributed ultimately to God, even if he acted through a human intermediary - 'drew me from the deadly pit' and its 'miry clay'. As is usually the case, we do not know the exact nature of the trouble that the psalmist faced, but the description offered, precisely because it is so vague, might fit any difficult or threatening situation in which we find ourselves, as well as the happy outcome. First an experience of something like a black, fetid pit, with no way out; and then the incredible rescue which leaves us feeling that at last 'my feet' are set 'upon a rock', so that henceforth 'my footsteps' are 'firm'. And even if our difficulties last a whole life through, we still have confidence to believe that we shall in the end find ourselves in secure rock-like safety.

'He put a new song into my mouth, praise of our God. Many shall see and fear and shall trust in the Lord.'

The rescue experienced by the psalmist would indeed invite 'a new song' of 'praise of our God'. Moreover, news of the remarkable rescue might well lead others first to 'see' and appreciate what God had done, then to 'fear' him (not so much in terror as in awe) and finally to 'trust in the Lord'. Faithfulness to the Good News, as today's gospel makes clear, may at times cost us dearly, but above all it inspires us to sing God's praises in such fashion that others may be led to share our joy.

'As for me, wretched and poor, the Lord thinks of me. You are my rescuer, my help, O God, do not delay.'

In addition to his testimony to God's goodness to him in the past, the psalmist also gives voice to his present need. Despite everything, he is still 'wretched and poor'; in the vocabulary of the psalms that is a way of expressing that he is one of the 'little ones' who know they cannot cope by themselves but remain in need of God's help. He is sure that help will be forthcoming because he knows that 'the Lord thinks of me', keeps me in mind the whole time, and he is also 'my rescuer', 'my help'. Nonetheless the psalmist pleads that God will 'not delay', a plea reminiscent of the familiar quip: 'Give me patience, Lord, but please hurry!' Significantly, the refrain for today's psalm is 'Lord, come to my aid!'; past help makes us all the more confident to call upon God in present troubles.

LET US PRAY: *We praise and thank you, O God, our everlasting help, that through your Son, Jesus, you have drawn us out of the pit of sin and alienation and made us into your sons and daughters.*

Twenty-First Sunday in Ordinary Time

The first reading (Isaiah 36:18-21) brings an oracle of encouragement to the people of Israel after their return from exile: Jerusalem, they are assured, is to be a centre which will attract not only Jews but people of all nations 'to witness my glory'.

The gospel (Luke 13:22-30) takes the first reading a stage further, indicating that membership of a particular community will not in itself ensure entrance through the 'narrow gate'; in the end it is not privilege but conversion that matters, and that applies to all people.

The letter to the Hebrews (12:5-7, 11-13) reminds us that if we claim to be God's children, we must expect to be treated as God's children, and that will include paternal discipline. It also means that we should behave as God's children, bearing 'fruit in peace and goodness'.

In its two brief verses, Psalm 116, the responsorial psalm for today, calls upon all nations to praise the Lord.

Prayerful Ponderings

'Go out to the whole world; proclaim the Good News.'
The refrain for today's psalm comes from the Gospel of Mark.
Mere membership of God's people is not in itself enough, nor will
it do simply to claim that 'we once ate and drank in your company'
(see today's gospel); we also have the mission of spreading the Good
News of God's love to all people. It has to be admitted that in times
gone by the Church's missionary activity was often marred by a
failure to respect the values in other religions and to recognise the
presence of God's grace to be found there. In its Decree on the
Missionary Activity of the Church (*Ad Gentes*), the Second Vatican
Council urged that Christians 'should with joy and reverence
discover the seeds of the Word which lie hidden in them [other,
non-Christian, religions]' (§11); however, it also insisted – in
Chapter I of the Decree – that 'The pilgrim Church is of its very
nature missionary, since it draws its origin from the mission of the
Son and the mission of the Holy Spirit, in accordance with the plan
of God the Father.'

**'O praise the Lord, all you nations; acclaim him all you
peoples!'**
The psalmist certainly had what we might call a missionary
outlook: he saw that 'praise [of] the Lord' must of course be the
special concern of God's people, but at the same time it must never

be regarded as their sole preserve; it is for the whole human race. And so this, the shortest psalm in the Psalter, is an invitation on the grandest possible scale, for it is addressed to 'all you nations' and to 'all you peoples', and it invites them to 'praise' and 'acclaim' the Lord. Until that happens God will not be recognised for what he is, the Lord of all; and until that happens, the nations will not enjoy their rightful place among his people.

'Strong is his love for us; he is faithful for ever.'

There are other psalms which give reasons why all people should praise the Lord, but usually those reasons are concerned with God's creative activity: it is he who made them, therefore they should worship him. In this psalm, somewhat unexpectedly, the reason offered is not creation but salvation. The appeal is to those two great covenant characteristics of God: the fact that 'his love' (*hesed*) is 'strong' and that his faithfulness (*emet*) is 'for ever'. What God has done for his people in the past, especially in the Exodus, and the love and faithfulness he has shown both then and ever since should serve to encourage other people to praise and serve him. It is fascinating to note that Paul himself quotes this psalm to show how Jesus has confirmed the hopes and promises of the past 'in order that the Gentiles might glorify God for his mercy' (Romans 15:9). And so as Christians we can make this psalm a prayer that the saving work accomplished by Christ may be proclaimed before the world by the way we live our lives and that that will in turn spur others to discover him and to praise the Lord of all. It is worth recalling the words of Pope John Paul II in *Redemptoris Missio*, the Encyclical he wrote to commemorate the 25th anniversary of *Ad Gentes*: 'Today', he wrote, 'as never before, the Church has the opportunity of bringing the Gospel, by witness and word, to all people and nations. I see the dawning of a new missionary age, which will become ... an abundant harvest, if all Christians ... respond with generosity and holiness to the calls and challenges of our time' (92).

LET US PRAY: *God of the universe, while acknowledging the action of your Holy Spirit among all peoples, we pray that we may not fail in our responsibility for the mission of the Church, so that people from east and west, from north and south, will come to know the Lord Jesus and one day take their places at the feast of the kingdom.*

Twenty-Second Sunday in Ordinary Time

The wise teacher of the first reading (Ecclesiasticus 3:17-20, 28-29) urges us to 'be gentle' and 'behave humbly' if we wish to 'find favour with the Lord'. At the same time, he warns that 'there is no cure for the proud'!

In the gospel (Luke 14:1, 7-14) Jesus urges us to choose 'the lowest place' and to offer hospitality not to the rich but to the poor, for in the kingdom those who exalt themselves will be humbled.

At Mount Sinai God revealed himself in awesome power, but, according to the second reading (Hebrews 12:18-19, 22-24), he has in Jesus revealed himself in humble form and taught us that our home is a new Jerusalem where 'everyone is a "first-born son [or daughter]"'.

The responsorial psalm is no more than a brief excerpt from Psalm 67, a lengthy song which has as its theme the march from Sinai through the desert wilderness to Jerusalem where God has his sanctuary and from where he rules Israel and all the nations. It sings of a God who is at once triumphant warrior and gentle Saviour of those in need.

Prayerful Ponderings

'The just shall rejoice at the presence of God, they shall exult and dance for joy. O sing to the Lord, make music to his name; rejoice in the Lord, exult at his presence.'

In the introductory couple of verses of this psalm (not included in today's responsorial psalm), God is called upon to arise in power and effortlessly scatter his enemies, as though they were smoke blown away by a breeze or wax melted by a fire. Then, the psalm turns to the response that his conquest will evoke among 'the just'. They 'shall rejoice' in his victory, and their rejoicing will not lack enthusiasm, for they will 'exult and dance for joy', as they celebrate what he has accomplished. It seems probable that in ancient times the psalm was sung as accompaniment to a festal procession which 'recreated' the victory of the Lord over his enemies and his triumphal entry into his sanctuary. The ark would be carried in the procession in order to signify his presence among the worshippers. All are called upon to join in the festivities, to 'make music to his name', 'to rejoice' in him and to 'exult at his presence'. Because of the victory the Lord Jesus has won for us, at the cost of his own life's blood, we have even more powerful reasons to rejoice, to sing and to make music to his name.

'Father of the orphan, defender of the widow, such is God in his holy place. God gives the lonely a home to live in; he leads the prisoners forth into freedom.'

But now comes an unexpected twist: the psalmist praises God not for his mighty victories over powerful enemies, but rather for his gentleness and concern for the weak and lowly ones. Long ago at the Exodus he had revealed himself by coming to the rescue of his people in their afflictions, and he has not changed in his attitude towards those in need. From 'his holy place', his lofty home in heaven, he bends down like a 'father of the orphan' and a 'defender of the widow'; orphans and widows were two of the most vulnerable categories of people in Israelite society. As father and as defender, he takes them in his special care and is active on their behalf. Similarly, the deliverance he has won includes provision for the homeless and restoration of liberty for 'the prisoners'.

'You poured down, O God, a generous rain; when your people were starved you gave them new life. It was there that your people found a home, prepared in your goodness, O God, for the poor.'

Again the psalmist's thoughts turn to the way God showed his love for his people during their desert days, working miracles on their behalf, like providing 'a generous rain' when they were parched with thirst, and the manna, which 'gave them new life', when they were starving with hunger. Similarly, at the end of their wanderings, when they were 'poor' and homeless, he provided 'a home' for his people in their own land; and all this was done out of his 'goodness'. The refrain to the psalm – 'In your goodness, O God, you prepared a home for the poor' – has taken this verse in slightly amended form as if to remind us, on the one hand, that God retains his concern for the poor and needy, and, on the other, that we are expected to imitate his 'humility' by acting towards others, especially the poor and lowly, as he has acted towards them – and us. If Israel was fortunate in having the Exodus as the convincing proof of God's love for them, we are more fortunate still: in the life, the death and the resurrection of Jesus we have still more vivid proof of God's love for the poor and the sinful. His victory was won not by mighty deeds but through the scandal of the cross; and it is in the power that his death has won for us that we, who so easily slip into pride, find strength to be humble and in particular to care for the least of our brothers and sisters.

LET US PRAY: *God of the poor, listen to us as we pray; help us to follow your example in concern for the poor and needy, and may we and they one day rejoice in the home that you have prepared for us in your goodness and where you reign with the Son and the Holy Spirit.*

Twenty-Third Sunday in Ordinary Time

The first reading (Wisdom 9:13-18) argues that because of our limitations, which it attributes to the fact that we are 'burdened' by the body, we can never understand the mind of God, and yet through his gift of wisdom we can come to the beginning of an understanding.

Since Jesus is the Wisdom of God incarnate, we must follow him, whatever renunciations that may entail, even those which may affect our dearest relatives and friends (Luke 14:25-33).

The slave Onesimus returns to his master with a request from Paul that he should be received back as 'a dear brother'. This is the wisdom of the gospel brought to bear in a practical situation (Philemon 9-10, 12-17).

The verses from Psalm 89 which make up today's responsorial psalm show that one vital ingredient of wisdom is the recognition of our own transience and God's eternity.

Prayerful Ponderings

'O Lord, you have been our refuge from one generation to the next.'

These words, which form the refrain of today's responsorial psalm, are the opening words of the psalm itself. They are an expression of confidence in the 'Lord', who has always proved himself to be 'our refuge'. Experience 'from one generation to the next' has shown that he can be relied upon. 'It is when faced with death' says, Vatican II (The Church in the Modern World §18), 'that the enigma of the human condition is most evident.' Yet, faced with that enigma, the psalmist proclaims that the Lord still gives us hope.

'You turn men back into dust and say: "Go back, sons of men." To your eyes a thousand years are like yesterday, come and gone, no more than a watch in the night.'

Together with confidence in God, there is also a readiness to face up to the reality of the human situation. The psalmist quickly begins to draw the contrast between, on the one hand, the eternity of him, in whose eyes 'a thousand years are like yesterday, come and gone', passing by as swiftly as does 'a watch in the night'; and, on the other, the transience of humankind, to whom he gives the order 'Go back, sons of men' into the native dust from which you came – an apparent allusion to Genesis 3:19.

'You sweep men away like a dream, like grass which springs up in the morning. In the morning it springs up and flowers: by evening it withers and fades.'

The finitude of our existence is graphically brought home by means of two examples: we are 'like a dream', says the psalmist, which lasts but a short while and then is swept away as though it had never existed; again, we are 'like grass', which 'in the morning' seems so full of promise, for then it 'springs up and flowers', but by the time 'evening' comes the truth is clear: the morning grass has no future: it simply 'withers and fades'. (However, it is Jesus who reminds us that if the Father clothes the grass of the field so beautifully, even though it is destined to feed tomorrow's oven, how much more he will do for you, 'you of little faith'! [Matthew 6:28-30].)

'Make us know the shortness of our life that we may gain wisdom of heart. Lord, relent! Is your anger for ever? Show pity to your servants.'

This verse is central to the psalm: even without any clear idea of eternal life, the psalmist recognises that facing up to 'the shortness of life' is of value in that it enables us to 'gain wisdom of heart', it helps us to see things in their true perspective. Nonetheless, the Lord is asked to 'relent' – literally to 'turn back'; earlier in the psalm he was pictured turning mortals back to dust, now he is asked to turn himself back to them again, in other words, to 'show pity to [his] servants' . Furthermore, he is asked if his 'anger' is to last for ever. Even when we accept the shortness of life, we may still beg to live a little longer; we are not ready just yet! Perhaps the psalm was composed at a time of particular distress or difficulty, so that along with a recognition of human transitoriness, there is an appeal for relief from present troubles.

'In the morning, fill us with your love; we shall exult and rejoice all our days. Let the favour of the Lord be upon us; give success to the work of our hands.'

In any event, the psalm ends as it began with a declaration of confidence. The Lord is confidently asked that 'in the morning' of a new day he will 'fill us with [his] love', allow his 'favour' to be focused 'upon us' and, despite the shortness of our life, to 'give success to the work of our hands'. With those favours granted 'we shall exult and rejoice', above all in God our Benefactor 'all our days'. As Christians, we know that 'life is a little gleam of time between two eternities' (Thomas Carlisle) and we rejoice that through the resurrection of Jesus we are able to look forward to 'sharing for ever a life that is divine and free from all decay' (The Church in the Modern World §18).

LET US PRAY: *Buoyed up by our belief that you are our strong refuge, we beg you, Lord of life and death, to give us courage to follow your Son, Jesus, wherever he may lead and whatever it may cost, and so may we rejoice all our days as we look forward to what you have prepared for those who love you.*

Twenty-Fourth Sunday in Ordinary Time

Like the prodigal son, the people of Israel deserted their God for the golden calf; but, through his spokesman, Moses, God showed that his forgiveness is greater than his children's unfaithfulness (Exodus 32:7-11, 13-14).

A shepherd seeking his lost sheep, a woman seeking her lost coin, a father seeking a lost son; all rejoice in finding what was lost, and all, but above all the father, reveal a glimpse of the welcome God gives sinners, his children who have gone astray (Luke 15:1-32).

Paul is able to rejoice because mercy was shown him and in that knowledge he proclaims the gospel of grace (1 Timothy 1:12-17).

It is hardly surprising that the verses that make up this Sunday's psalm should come from one of the seven 'penitential psalms', in fact from the most popular of them all, Psalm 50.

Prayerful Ponderings

'I will leave this place and go to my father.'
These words, which form the refrain of the responsorial psalm, come from Luke 15:18; they mark the point at which the prodigal son, having reached rock bottom, comes to himself and decides that he must return to his father, acknowledge his guilt and if need be accept a position as one of his 'father's paid servants'. In fact he was received with a warmth and a forgiveness which went far beyond anything he could ever have imagined (see today's gospel). And that is how the Lord always receives those who return to him.

'Have mercy on me, God, in your kindness. In your compassion blot out my offence. O wash me more and more from my guilt and cleanse me from my sins.'
The opening words of the psalm provide a brief theology of sin. First, they offer three terms for sin, each of them highlighting one of its different aspects: an 'offence' (*pesha'* = to rebel), 'guilt' (*hatta'* = to miss the mark), and 'sin' ('*awon* = to be crooked, perverted). Secondly, they also describe the process of forgiveness by three different terms, as they beg God to 'blot out' my wrongdoing (so that it will no longer be remembered against me), to 'wash me more and more' (like garments that are trodden underfoot in the washing process) and to 'cleanse me from my sins' (like a person being washed clean of leprosy). Thirdly, they speak of two of the

outstanding attributes of God which lead him to forgive and to which the psalmist makes appeal: 'your kindness' (*hesed* = his faithful covenant love) and 'your compassion' (*rahamim* = a love like that of a mother for her child). All today's readings take on a deeper meaning when read against the backcloth of this extraordinary psalm; its impact on Christian theology and practice has been incalculable.

'A pure heart create for me, O God, put a steadfast spirit within me. Do not cast me away from your presence, nor deprive me of your holy spirit.'

Again the psalmist shows fine theological acumen by declaring in effect that a 'pure heart' is not something that we can make for ourselves; it is rather God's own creation; the word used for 'create' (*bara*) is used exclusively of God in the language of the Hebrew Bible. Similarly, it is God alone who can 'put' within us that 'steadfast spirit' which will enable us to be faithful to him in the future. That conviction leads into the plea that he will never 'cast me away' and never 'deprive me of [his] holy spirit'. Whatever the psalmist had in mind, we must surely want to make this a prayer to the Holy Spirit, the Paraclete that Jesus promised to his followers to continue and complete his own ministry, to guide them in his ways and lead them to the truth. (In John's Gospel the Paraclete appears on no fewer than five occasions during our Lord's final discourse to his disciples.)

'O Lord, open my lips and my mouth shall declare your praise. My sacrifice is a contrite spirit; a humbled, contrite heart you will not spurn.'

After the confession of sin, the expression of trust in God's mercy and the prayer for a pure heart and a steadfast spirit, the psalmist knows that there must be prayers of praise, too. However, even that is not possible without God's help, and so he begs him to 'open my lips and [I] shall declare your praise'. Today's psalm comes to an end with words that sum up all that has gone before: 'a contrite spirit' is in God's sight like a 'sacrifice' and 'a humbled, contrite heart [he] will not spurn'.

LET US PRAY: *It is hard to find words, gracious Father, to express our gratitude for the loving way you deal with those who return to you, despite their rebellions, going astray and perversity; may we, never doubting your readiness to forgive, be among those who, through repentance, bring joy to the angels in heaven.*

Twenty-Fifth Sunday in Ordinary Time

Amos, from Tekoa, a small town south of Jerusalem, is the first prophet whose message has come down to us in the form of a book. It is a fierce message, condemning social injustice: those who trample on the needy cannot serve God (Amos 8:4-7).

The gospel reinforces the message of Amos, though in a less aggressive way: Jesus speaks of a wily steward who shows more ingenuity in pursuit of earthly goods than 'the children of light' show in pursuit of spiritual concerns (Luke 16:1-13).

Paul urges us to pray for all people but especially for those in positions of political authority; they have the special responsibility of care for the poor and the preservation of peace (1 Timothy 2:1-8).

Today's psalm comes from Psalm 112, the first of a group known as the 'Hallel (= praise the Lord) psalms' which were sung on the great festival days of Passover, Weeks and Tabernacles. It praises God in particular because of the care he shows for the lowly people.

Prayerful Ponderings

'Praise, O servants of the Lord, praise the name of the Lord! May the name of the Lord be blessed both now and for evermore!'

The first word of this psalm sets the tone: it is a summons to 'praise … the name of the Lord'. But a name is more than a mere label: in Hebrew thought it stands for a person's innermost being, an individual's essential self; it has a mysterious identity with the one who bears it. Praise is of its nature directed towards God: it is given him precisely because he is God and therefore deserving of it. Those to whom the summons is directed are the 'servants of the Lord', those specially chosen as his own, and their response is to acknowledge him, using the name – 'Lord' (Yahweh) – by which he revealed himself to Moses (Exodus 3). But because he is a Lord who transcends the limits of time, the plea is that he should be praised for all time, 'blessed both now and for evermore'. (It was traditional for the first two of the Hallel psalms [112 and 113] to be sung at the end of the paschal meal. And so it was with this psalm of praise on his lips that Jesus left the Upper Room and went towards his passion.)

'High above all nations is the Lord, above the heavens his glory. Who is like the Lord, our God, who has risen on high to his throne, yet stoops from the heights to look down, to look down upon heaven and earth?'

'The Lord' is quite simply incomparable. 'High above all nations', not only is he superior to every earthly power, 'his glory' – the splendour and power which belong to him by right – places him 'above the heavens', and all that they contain. The psalm goes on to speak of a unique characteristic of Israel's God: not only 'has [he] risen on high to his throne', he also 'stoops' down low. The psalmist cannot resist the question: 'Who is like the Lord, our God', who of the so-called gods of the other nations ever did anything like that? This simple yet delightful picture of God as one who, though dwelling on high, 'stoops' down low in concern for his people and the world he made, is a stage in a revelation that will reach its climax in the person of Jesus Christ, champion of the sick, of the poor, of the outcast, and, for that very reason, opponent of every type of social injustice (see today's readings).

'From the dust he lifts up the lowly, from the dungheap he raises the poor, to set him in the company of princes, yes, with the princes of his people.'
The refrain of today's psalm – 'Praise the Lord, who raises the poor' – is based upon this verse and clearly captures the essence of the psalm. Our God is particularly deserving of praise because he shows such concern for the poor, in complete contrast to those people excoriated by Amos (first reading) whose sole concern was to exploit the poor, make a good turn-over and fill their own pockets. It might be said that it is rather dangerous to pray Psalm 112, as we are invited to do this Sunday, for how can we pray it with integrity unless we recognise that we as the servants of the Lord are meant to put flesh on this psalm in our daily living?

LET US PRAY: *Great God, who stoops so low out of love for the poor and needy, we praise and bless your name, but we also plead that our prayers may be translated into deeds as we strive to help our sisters and brothers in their needs.*

Twenty-Sixth Sunday in Ordinary Time

The eighth century prophet Amos preaches to the prosperous Israelites, chiding them for their failure to appreciate the needs of the poor and warning them that they will be the first to be forced into exile (Amos 6:1, 4-7)

The gospel has a similar message: the rich man has insulated himself from the desperate condition of the poor man, Lazarus; but death will bring a terrifying reversal of fortune (Luke 16:19-31).

The first letter to Timothy (6:11-16) exhorts us to 'fight the good fight' and persevere in living up to the demands of the Christian life until 'the Appearing of our Lord Jesus Christ'. A vital part of our Christian obligation is to come to the help of the needy.

Psalm 145 stands at the head of a final group of psalms of praise which brings the Psalter to a close. The verses chosen for today's responsorial psalm highlight the fact that the poor and oppressed are the ones who benefit most from the power and faithfulness of the Lord.

Prayerful Ponderings

'My soul, give praise to the Lord.'
These are the introductory words of Psalm 145; they are a call to 'praise the Lord', but this time a call with a difference since it is directed, rather unusually, to the psalmist, rather than to others: it is 'my soul', and that means myself, that receives the call. And of course in today's liturgy we too are expected to invite our soul (ourselves) to bestir itself and joyously praise the Lord.

'It is the Lord who keeps faith for ever, who is just to those who are oppressed. It is he who gives bread to the hungry, the Lord, who sets prisoners free.'
The psalm certainly begins as a hymn of praise, but almost immediately shades into a psalm of instruction. 'The Lord' himself is set before us as the One who can always be relied upon, for he 'keeps faith for ever'; above all he is faithful in his special love and concern for those who are less fortunate in life. So he 'is just to those who are oppressed' in any way, he 'gives bread to the hungry' and 'sets prisoners free'. His way of dealing with the poor stands in startling contrast to that of so many of the wealthy people of this world (see first reading and gospel); it also stands as a challenge to all who claim to belong to him. St Gregory the Great reminds us that: 'When we attend to the needs of those in want, we give them what is theirs, not ours. More than performing works of mercy, we are paying a debt of justice.'

'It is the Lord who gives sight to the blind, who raises up those who are bowed down. It is the Lord who loves the just, the Lord, who protects the stranger.'

The description of the Lord's generosity to the needy continues. He 'gives sight to the blind' and 'raises up those who are bowed down' with troubles of every kind, not always of course by restoring physical vision or removing heavy burdens but often by giving those who are physically blind an insight into things and an appreciation of them which sighted people do not always possess, or by enabling those who have to contend with great troubles to grow and mature as human beings in and through their problems.

'He upholds the widow and orphan but thwarts the path of the wicked.'

In earlier verses many of the traditional 'corporal works of mercy' were mentioned, but the psalmist could hardly fail to make specific mention of care for 'the widow and orphan'. Widows and orphans, together with 'the stranger' (see previous verse), were almost a standard expression in biblical times for the vulnerable members of society: those without a husband or without parents (or without a foothold in the land) faced particular hardships, often depending upon the good will of others if they were to survive. These, says the psalmist, are the very ones whom the Lord 'upholds'. Jesus shared that viewpoint (see today's gospel) and unhesitatingly identified himself with the least of his brothers and sisters; and, despite the failings of many of her members, the Church has always worked for the relief, defence and liberation of those in need, regarding them as the object of her preferential love. We cannot fail to notice that according to the psalmist 'the wicked', and in this context that must mean those who ignore the poor, cannot expect God's favour; indeed he 'thwarts the path' of such people. It would be hard to think of a more salutary warning for ourselves in view of the fact that we have heard not only Moses and the prophets but also someone who has risen from the dead (see the gospel), Jesus our Saviour; we of all people have least excuse for failure in this area.

'The Lord will reign for ever, Zion's God, from age to age.'
At the beginning of the psalm we were reminded that God is faithful for ever, in the intervening verses we were given a thumbnail sketch, as it were, of the characteristic ways in which he shows his faithfulness, and now at the end we are told that he 'will reign for ever … from age to age'. When we feel overwhelmed by the high expectations that the Lord has of us, it might be helpful to recall that we are not asked to do anything in our own power: it is he who 'will reign for ever', it is he who is 'God', and it is he, if we will let him, who will enable us to imitate his own deep concern for the poor.

LET US PRAY: *Your Son, all-powerful God, showed to others your ever-faithful concern for the poor and lowly; may the Good News of the Gospel be revealed through us to the poor, the hungry, the oppressed, the prisoner and the needy.*

Twenty-Seventh Sunday in Ordinary Time

To the prophet who wants to know 'How long am I to cry for help?', the Lord offers no answer but simply insists that the just person lives by faith (Habakkuk 1:2-3; 2:2-4).

Jesus also speaks of faith (Luke 17:5-9), commenting that it can achieve the moving of mountains but also noting that believers who live out their faith are doing no more than fulfilling their duty.

The passage from the second letter to Timothy (1:6-8, 13-14) also has implications for faith. Faith is never possessed definitively but must be continually aroused, especially in times of difficulty and trial.

As we saw a few weeks ago (see Eighteenth Sunday in Ordinary Time), Psalm 94 is an enthronement psalm, used in a liturgy which proclaimed the kingship of God.

Prayerful Ponderings

'Come, ring out our joy to the Lord; hail the rock who saves us. Let us come before him, giving thanks, with songs let us hail the Lord.'

Nothing so fills us with 'joy' as meeting the person we love; indeed, even the anticipation of such a meeting is already a cause of delight. Those who sang this psalm, as they made their way to the Temple, were people of faith; it was in the strength of that faith that they believed that they would soon be in the very presence of 'the Lord', and so, in approaching that meeting, they wanted only to 'ring out [their] joy', 'to come before him, giving thanks', and to 'hail' him 'with songs', the more so because they recognised him as their Saviour God, the sure 'rock' of their salvation. Jesus, our Saviour, promised his friends a very special joy; as he spoke of his desire 'that my joy may be in you, and that your joy may be full' (John 15:11). It is especially in the fact that he is risen and remains with us 'till the end of time' that Christian joy has its roots. It is a joy which should be deeply felt as we come to our weekly eucharistic meeting with our risen Lord.

'Come in, let us bow and bend low; let us kneel before the God who made us, for he is our God and we the people who belong to his pasture, the flock that is led by his hand.'

The psalmist and his companions felt the need to express their faith, their joy and their worship not only in words but in action, too. And so the call goes out: as we enter the Temple, 'let us bow', let us 'bend low', 'let us kneel'. The enthusiastic approach of our ancestors in the faith might well encourage us not to underestimate those actions that we are expected to perform: the blessing with holy water, the genuflection, the sign of peace, the standing for the gospel, etc. We are not simply souls but body-souls, and our whole being is meant to give expression to our faith. Those who first sang this hymn were particularly conscious that the God whom they worshipped was their Creator, 'the God who made us', but also their Shepherd, the God who cared for them, pastured them and 'led' them as his 'flock' from captivity to freedom. We too, as Christians, acknowledge that God is not only our Creator but also our Shepherd, our Good Shepherd, leading us from the slavery of sin to the freedom of the children to God, and ultimately to eternal life and perfect happiness.

'O that today you would listen to his voice! "Harden not your hearts as at Meribah, as on that day at Massah in the desert when your fathers put me to the test; when they tried me, though they saw my work."'

The refrain for today's psalm highlights the importance of listening to God's voice and responding to it: 'O that today you would listen to his voice! "Harden not your hearts".'

Where there is faith, there also is the desire to do God's will, to 'listen to his voice', to render him what St Paul calls 'the obedience of faith' (Romans 1:5). Put negatively, as those who first sang this hymn realised, we are not to follow the example of those who were present at 'Meribah' and 'Massah', two places in the desert wilderness for ever associated with rebellion against God; there, the people refused to 'listen to his voice'; they 'tried' him and 'put [him] to the test'. And so the psalmist pleads that the lesson of history will not be forgotten by his contemporaries. Centuries later, the author of the letter to the Hebrews (3:7-19) insisted that this text is meant for us when it speaks of the obligation to obey God's will, to 'listen to his voice'. And more recently still, the *Catechism of the Catholic Church* draws attention to this verse of the psalm, stressing the importance of 'today'. Each 'today' of our lives God is with us in a variety of ways, not only when we pray or attend religious services but in all the events of daily life. '(I)t is in the present', says the Catechism, 'that we encounter him, not yesterday nor tomorrow, but today' (§2659).

LET US PRAY: *Deepen our faith, Lord our God, so that we may more clearly recognise you in all the events of life and find our joy in listening and responding to your voice.*

Twenty-Eighth Sunday in Ordinary Time

Naaman, the Syrian general (2 Kings 5:14-17), is cured of leprosy and in gratitude takes home with him some of the earth of Israel, a tangible reminder of the Promised Land, so that henceforth he may worship the one true God of Israel – on Israel's own soil!

The gospel also tells of the cure of a leper, in fact of ten lepers, but only one, and he a Samaritan, had the good grace to return and give thanks (Luke 17:11-19).

Paul (2 Timothy 2:8-13) is confident that 'God's news' cannot be chained: as the other readings show, God's blessings reach out beyond the Chosen People to non-Israelites.

Psalm 97 is another of the enthronement psalms, hymns celebrating the universal kingship of God. The verses chosen for today's psalm show how his saving power is not restricted to Israel but stretches out to all people, everywhere.

Prayerful Ponderings

'Sing a new song to the Lord for he has worked wonders. His right hand and his holy arm have brought salvation.'

'A new song' of praise is called for in recognition of the way in which 'the Lord' has shown his sovereign power. As his people well know, 'he has worked wonders' for them ever since he rescued them from slavery in Egypt, the word 'wonders' implying that the interventions were nothing short of the miraculous. 'His right hand and his holy arm' – again, the words suggest the divine identity of the warrior who fought on their behalf – guided them through the desert wilderness and led them into their own land. He 'brought them salvation'.

'The Lord has made known his salvation; has shown his justice to the nations.'

However, the emphasis is not so much on the recipients of 'his salvation' but on 'the Lord' himself who accomplished it, and on the fact that what he has done has been witnessed by all 'the nations'. He has revealed to all the world his 'justice', his ability to set right what was wrong, in favour of his people. Moreover, as today's readings remind us, God's saving work has not simply been witnessed by the nations: it has actually overflowed to them, in the persons of the non-Israelite Naaman, and of the Samaritan who was a leper. The refrain of today's psalm – 'The Lord has shown his salvation to the nations' – reflects this verse and the astonishing belief that lies behind it: that what God has done for his chosen people in their history is a revelation of his universal rule throughout the course of human history and of all that he has done for humanity.

'He has remembered his truth and love for the house of Israel.'
Memory is at the heart of biblical religion. If, on his side, God 'has remembered' his covenant commitment to 'the house of Israel' by an unfailing show of 'truth' (faithfulness) and 'love', they, on their side, are expected to remember him and all that he has done for them, and so be filled with gratitude. It was because Naaman remembered and was truly grateful that, after his cure, he returned to Elisha and said, 'Now I know that there is no God in all the earth except in Israel. Now, please, accept a present from your servant.' He even took back with him some of Israel's soil, a permanent keepsake. Similarly, it was because the Samaritan remembered his cure that he 'turned back praising God at the top of his voice'. And of course at the heart of our Christian faith also there is remembrance and gratitude, for every Mass, the re-presentation of the saving activity of the Lord, is celebrated 'in memory of me', and every Mass is Eucharist, a service of thanksgiving.

'All the ends of the earth have seen the salvation of our God. Shout to the Lord, all the earth, ring out your joy.'
For the third time in this brief psalm the word 'salvation' is heard, together with a reference to 'all the ends of the earth', leaving the unmistakable impression that the psalm is somehow straining forward towards what the future will bring. One day a Child will

be born whose name means 'God saves' (Matthew 1:21, 25). Even before his birth, his mother's spirit will rejoice because of the 'great things' that God has done for her and because, through the coming of her son, God 'is [still] remembering his mercy' (Luke 1:54), he is being true to his covenant alliance with his people, with all that that means in terms of love, compassion, friendship, mercy. This Child will indeed bring salvation to the ends of the earth and 'of his kingdom there will be no end' (Luke 1:33). For Jesus, and for all that his coming has brought to the human race, we can gratefully make the psalmist's cry our own: 'Shout to the Lord, all the earth, ring out your joy.'

LET US PRAY: *It is in a spirit of joy and gratitude that we come before you today, great and mighty God. We thank you for the wonders that you have worked for us and for the whole human race through your Son, Jesus Christ, our Lord.*

Twenty-Ninth Sunday in Ordinary Time

So long as Moses remains with arms outstretched in prayer, Israel remains victorious against the enemy (Exodus 17:8-13).

Perseverance in prayer is the subject of the gospel, also. Such perseverance, born of faith, is especially needed when God seems to be silent (Luke 18:1-8).

The second letter to Timothy (3:14 – 4:2) teaches that a vital aspect of faith is recognition of the divinely inspired nature of Scripture; only then will we be able to proclaim the living gospel – Jesus Christ.

Psalm 120 is the second of the Songs of Ascent, a group of psalms used by pilgrims as they made their way up (their ascent) to Jerusalem for the three great feast days.

Prayerful Ponderings

'I lift up my eyes to the mountains: from where shall come my help? My help shall come from the Lord who made heaven and earth.'

The psalm begins with what seems to be a dialogue, though it is not clear with whom the psalmist is speaking: is it a companion? A priest? Himself (so that it's a kind of soliloquy, the question being simply rhetorical)? In any event, as he draws close to Jerusalem, the psalmist raises 'my eyes to the mountains', amidst which the holy city is set. Aware of the dangers that may lie ahead, from wild animals, from robbers, from difficult terrain, he asks the anxious question: 'from where shall come my help?', and back comes the confident reply: 'from the Lord who made heaven and earth'. The confession of God as Creator of heaven and earth eventually found its way into the Apostles' Creed, but already in this psalm it underlines the limitless power of the 'help' that is forthcoming 'from the Lord'. It is no surprise that the refrain for today's psalm should be taken from this verse: 'Our help is in the name of the Lord who made heaven and earth.'

'May he never allow you to stumble! Let him sleep not, your guard. No, he sleeps not nor slumbers, Israel's guard.'

Having confessed his confidence in the Lord, the psalmist goes on to explain how utterly God can be relied upon. There may be those who would cynically say: 'It's to be hoped he won't "allow you to stumble" on your journey, it's to be hoped he doesn't fall asleep, this guard of yours!' To such questionings of the Lord's reliability, the psalmist's response is that 'Israel's guard' is quite unlike any other, for he is never off duty, he never 'sleeps' or 'slumbers'; he is always alert to protect his people. (It calls to mind the way Elijah taunted the prophets of Baal, suggesting that the reason fire didn't come down from heaven at their request was because, in striking contrast to the God of Israel, 'perhaps he [Baal] is asleep and must be awakened' [1 Kings 18:27]!)

'The Lord is your guard and your shade; at your right side he stands. By day the sun shall not smite you nor the moon in the night.'

The word 'guard', which appeared twice in the previous verse, is repeated here, and will be repeated again in the subsequent verses. It stands as a key idea of the psalm and its constant repetition – as well as the repetition of other words, such as 'sleep' and 'slumber' – gives the prayer what has been called a 'stair-like' quality, one verse, or part of a verse, leading up to the next. It is because the Lord is your guardian that he stands as 'your shade … at your right side': a warrior carrying his shield on his left hand would be unprotected on the right side of his body, were it not for his companion who stood as his shade and protector on that side. Again, it is because the Lord is your guardian that you will come to no harm when you are abroad night or day: so 'the sun shall not smite you', despite its broiling heat 'by day'; nor during 'the night' will you come to any harm from 'the moon', often associated with dangerous influences (because of course your guard never sleeps!).

'The Lord will guard you from evil, he will guard your soul. The Lord will guard your going and coming both now and for ever.'

The psalmist concludes his prayer by once against asserting, but now it would seem with even greater confidence, that 'the Lord will guard you from [every] evil', he 'will guard your [every] going and coming both now and for ever'. In our own pilgrim journey through life we have Jesus' own assurance that he is our guardian, our 'Good Shepherd' who always cares for his sheep, so that 'No one will snatch them out of my hand' (John 10:28). In the last resort it is only trust in the Lord that will give us courage to persevere in prayer, even in those dark times when it seems to go unheard.

LET US PRAY: *Lord Jesus Christ, you have assured us that you have prepared a place for us in your Father's house. Help us on our pilgrimage journey, protect us from every evil, keep us always faithful to prayer and enable us to persevere to the end.*

Thirtieth Sunday in Ordinary Time

Sirach, the author of today's first reading (Ecclesiasticus 35:12-14, 16-19), teaches that God in his justice has a special care for the oppressed and the powerless.

In the gospel it is the tax collector who goes home 'at rights with God' because he is humble enough to acknowledge his sinfulness; he is a poor man who comes to God with empty hands, depending on his mercy (Luke 18:9-14).

In the second reading Paul is presented as one who while aware of his achievement – 'I have fought the good fight to the end … I have kept the faith' – is still more aware that it would have been impossible without the Lord's help, and so his prayer is one of thanksgiving to the Lord who has always 'stood by me' (2 Timothy 4:6-8, 16-18).

The verses from the thanksgiving psalm, Psalm 33, which make up today's responsorial psalm are particularly appropriate, for they focus on the fate of those who are 'poor' and who cry to God for his help.

Prayerful Ponderings

'This poor man called; the Lord heard him.'
This verse, which is the refrain to today's psalm, indicates that the psalmist himself, spoken of (rather coyly) in the third person, is a 'poor man' and that he has himself had the experience of answered prayer: it was when he 'called' in prayer that 'the Lord heard him'. The Hebrew word for 'poor' (*'ani*) is derived from a verb which means 'to be bowed down, to be afflicted'. The image of someone bent double with affliction makes it easy to understand how the word came to cover the whole gamut of hardship situations, such as poverty, servitude, sterility, weakness, oppression. However, in the course of their history, and especially under the guidance of the prophets, the people came to a surprising conviction: that God has a special care for people when they are in a state of humiliation. It is a conviction shared by the psalmist. (It is not so much a case of exalting poverty in itself, as of highlighting God's concern for the poor and of. urging us to follow his example.)

'I will bless the Lord at all times, his praise always on my lips; in the Lord my soul shall make its boast. The humble shall hear and be glad.'
The psalm is an invocation of praise and thanksgiving from the psalmist ('I will bless the Lord at all times'). The singer of the psalm is able to say that God's 'praise [is] always on my lips', that it is 'in

the Lord' that 'my soul [= "myself"] shall makes its boast'; while the other worshippers, when they 'hear' about it, share in his joy, they too are 'glad' and, presumably, follow his example. The Hebrew word for 'the humble' (*'anawim*) originally had much the same meaning as that for 'the poor' (see previous verse), but increasingly, and especially in the psalms, acquired a spiritual sense, so that it was almost synonymous with the pious, the devout, the humble (like the tax collector in the gospel), and the expression *'anawim* came to mean 'the poor of Yahweh'.

'The Lord turns his face against the wicked to destroy their remembrance from the earth. The just call and the Lord hears and rescues them in all their distress.'

This verse seems to claim that the good will always be rescued from their troubles, while the wicked will always get their come-uppance. However, it is perhaps less naïve than it sounds; ultimately, it is an expression of confidence in God. If 'the Lord' is said to turn 'his face against the wicked', those who oppress the poor and the weak, that is a way of saying that in the long run they cannot succeed, they are cutting themselves off from God's help and to that extent courting disaster. On the other hand, if it is said that 'the Lord hears [the just] and rescues them in all their distress', whenever they 'call' on him, that is a way of saying that their prayer will never go unheard. Such an outlook must have been difficult to sustain in times when there was little explicit belief in eternal life. For us Christians, however, it should be different, for we believe in an afterlife, we believe that the Lord 'will repay according to each one's deeds' (Romans 2:6): ultimately people will get the reward they have earned.

'The Lord is close to the broken-hearted; those whose spirit is crushed he will save. The Lord ransoms the souls of his servants. Those who hide in him shall not be condemned.'

Once again, this is an affirmation of faith in the Lord's concern for the poor: he 'is close to the broken-hearted', saves 'those whose spirit is crushed', 'ransoms' those who are 'his servants'. This is not the promise of an 'easy' life for such people, but rather the conviction that whatever comes their way, what really matters is the Lord's closeness to them; and it may well be that it is it in times of adversity that they become most keenly aware of his nearness and of what his help means. And so the wonderful final acclamation: 'Those who hide in him shall not be condemned', a foreshadowing of St Paul's assurance: 'There is therefore now no condemnation for those who are in Christ Jesus' (Romans 8:1).

LET US PRAY: *God, our Father, in your sight we are all poor and needy; as we thank you for your continual loving care, we pray that like the tax collector we may place all our trust in you so that one day we may reach our eternal home at rights with God.*

Thirty-First Sunday
in Ordinary Time

God loves all that he has made, says the book of Wisdom (11:22 – 12:2); he does not wish that sinners should perish but rather than they should come to repentance.

Zacchaeus, a despised tax collector, is converted and made rich in God's sight as he responds to Jesus' initiative (Luke 19:1-10).

Paul instructs his friends in Thessalonica that, without getting over-excited by the Lord's promised return in glory, they should recognise that even now by faith they are sharers in the salvation achieved for us by Christ (2 Thessalonians 1:11 – 2:2).

The verses from Psalm 144 selected for today's psalm praise and thank God for the universality of his care for his creatures. According to the Jewish Talmud, anyone who recites this psalm three times a day is 'certainly a child of the world to come'!

Prayerful Ponderings

'I will give you glory, O God my King, I will bless your name for ever. I will bless you day after day and praise your name for ever.'

This psalm is alphabetical in that each verse begins with a successive letter of the Hebrew alphabet, though unfortunately that feature is lost in the English translation. However, it is clear that this song of praise is addressed to God in particular because he cares for everything he has made – everything from A to Z, as we might say. It begins with the psalmist's repeated pledge to praise and bless and glorify God, whom he styles 'my King': 'I will give you glory', the psalmist says, 'I will bless your name for ever', 'I will bless you day after day.' It is the kind of prayer that Zacchaeus might well have made his own. The example of the psalmist sets an inspiring standard: to praise and exalt our God every day and all our days and for ever. The refrain to today's psalm – 'I will bless your name for ever, O God my King' – is clearly based on this verse.

'The Lord is kind and full of compassion, slow to anger, abounding in love. How good is the Lord to all, compassionate to all his creatures.'

The words of this verse, taken almost verbatim from Exodus 34:6 where God revealed himself to Moses, stress the Lord's 'compassion' and his 'abounding … love', which make him 'slow to anger' or, to express the same idea more positively, quick to show mercy and forgive (as Zacchaeus joyfully discovered). The reference to God's goodness 'to all', and his compassion for 'all his creatures' once again reflects the universality of outlook of the other readings.

'**All your creatures shall thank you, O Lord, and your friends shall repeat their blessing. They shall speak of the glory of your reign and declare your might, O God.**'

It is in response to the universality of the Lord's compassion and goodness that 'all [his] creatures ... thank you, O Lord'. However, a distinction has to be made: while his other creatures give him thanks simply by being what they are and functioning as they are, and while human beings should thank him, too, yet they must make a choice: they are not compelled to thank him. The sad fact is that it is not everybody but only 'your friends' who bless God with gratitude, who 'speak of the glory of your reign' and 'declare your might'. It was one of those friends of his, the German Dominican mystic Johannes Eckhart, who made the thought-provoking statement: 'If the only prayer you say in your whole life is "thank you" that would suffice.'

'**The Lord is faithful in all his words and loving in all his deeds. The Lord supports all who fall and raises all who are bowed down.**'

Yet again the universality of the Lord's goodness is highlighted: he 'is faithful in all his words', always keeps his promises; he is 'loving in all his deeds', all his actions are motivated by love and all his creatures are the beneficiaries of that love; he 'supports all who fall', especially those who fall foul of sin, and so he was ready 'to stay at a sinner's house' (gospel); he 'raises all who are bowed down', his almighty power is put at the disposal of the needy and distressed.

LET US PRAY: *Lord God, you show your goodness and love to all your creatures; may we be truly grateful and may we show our gratitude in a practical way by striving to be always compassionate and loving in our dealings with others.*

Thirty-Second Sunday in Ordinary Time

The first reading, taken from the second book of Maccabees (7:1-2, 9-14), tells of the valiant mother who, strong in her faith in the resurrection, encouraged her seven sons to suffer martyrdom rather than prove unfaithful.

In the gospel Jesus responds to the Sadducees, who had tried to ridicule him for his belief in the resurrection of the body, by explaining that they had not even begun to understand the transformation that will take place in the world of the resurrection (Luke 20:27-38).

While asking for the support of their prayers, Paul also begs the Christians of Thessalonica to pray with him that they may remain faithful to the love of God (2 Thessalonians 2:16 – 3:5).

Psalm 16, from which today's responsorial psalm is drawn, is a prayer of trust in God but also an appeal to him for deliverance from enemies who have wrongfully accused the psalmist.

Prayerful Ponderings

'Lord, hear a cause that is just, pay heed to my cry. Turn your ear to my prayer: no deceit is on my lips. I kept my feet firmly in your paths; there was no faltering in my steps.'

This is a psalm which may not come too easily to our lips; we may be put off by the self-righteous tone that seems to be adopted by the psalmist: my 'cause is just', there is 'no deceit on my lips', 'I kept my feet firmly in your paths', with 'no faltering in my steps'. However, this declaration of innocence is not as crude or as boastful as it sounds; it is no more a claim to sinlessness than were the protestations of Job (see chapter 31). In fact it is probably nothing more than a formal way of proclaiming 'not guilty' in the face of false accusations, a way of saying: I leave my cause with God; he knows the truth, let him punish me if he finds me guilty. And so the psalmist pleads that God will 'hear [my] cause' and 'pay heed to my cry'.

'I am here and I call, you will hear me, O God. Turn your ear to me; hear my words.'

Having testified to his or her innocence before God, the singer of the psalm now makes a direct appeal for help. There is something rather touching in the simple statement of fact: 'I am here and I call', coupled with the confident affirmation: 'you will hear me, O God'. In the face of such confidence, the petition – 'Turn your ear to me; hear my words' – hardly seems necessary, and yet in times of great difficulty it is not at all unusual for protestations of utter confidence to be linked with reiterated cries for help: that is the way that human beings behave.

'Guard me as the apple of your eye. Hide me in the shadow of your wings.'

The beautiful words of the first sentence, which in Deuteronomy 32:10 are applied to the whole people of God, are here applied to an individual member of that community. In Hebrew the word for 'apple of [one's] eye' means literally 'a little man', referring to the way in which the eye's pupil reflects a tiny image of someone standing close by. What an attractive way of affirming the intimacy and tenderness of God and our mutual closeness! Similarly, the image of sheltering 'in the shadow of your wings' was used originally of the whole people (see Deuteronomy 32:11) but is now used to indicate God's protective closeness to the psalmist.

'As for me, in my justice I shall see your face and be filled, when I awake, with the sight of your glory.'

This psalm, brimming with confidence in God, must have been the kind of prayer which sustained the Maccabean mother when she strove to encourage her sons in their hour of trial. It seems likely that the latter part of this verse, which incidentally also serves as the refrain to today's psalm – 'I shall be filled, when I awake, with the sight of your glory' – was understood by the psalmist in terms of this earth's life. There was a custom of spending a night in prayer in the Temple with the hope that in the morning, regarded as a propitious time for God's favours, the worshipper, who suffered from sickness, for example, would be rewarded with restoration to health. However, even if the original psalmist was unaware of it, this psalm already carried a hint of an even greater truth, the truth that had already become more widely accepted in the time of the Maccabees (second century BC) and was finally and fully revealed in the resurrection of Jesus Christ. Through his resurrection we are given the mighty hope that the dead are 'children of the resurrection', that beyond this life we look forward to 'the sight of your glory', when 'we will see him as he is' (1 John 3:2).

LET US PRAY: *Lord God of the living, your Son, Jesus Christ, 'holy, innocent and undefiled', was unjustly condemned to death, but you raised him in the glory of the resurrection. We pray for the final vindication of all the innocent people in our times who suffer imprisonment, torture and death.*

Thirty-Third Sunday in Ordinary Time

If Jesus' birth marked the Day of the Lord, the prophet Malachi (3:19-20) reminds us that there will be another Day of the Lord, when he comes again; it will be a day of judgement.

As we await the coming of the Lord, says Paul (2 Thessalonians 3:7-12), we must not slide either into anxiety or into laziness, but work conscientiously at our daily tasks.

Jesus describes the Day of the Lord in terms of catastrophic happenings but also gives his disciples the assurance that they will be cared for so long as they persevere (Luke 21:5-19).

Psalm 97 is an enthronement psalm, trumpeting God's sovereign rule over all the nations. The latter part of the psalm, which is today's responsorial psalm, invites even inanimate nature to hail 'the Lord who comes'.

Prayerful Ponderings

'Sing psalms to the Lord with the harp, with the sound of music. With trumpets and the sound of the horn acclaim the King, the Lord.'

The first part of this psalm, which does not feature in today's responsorial psalm, proclaimed the saving work of God; now the liturgical choir is asked to celebrate what he has done, to 'sing psalms [of praise] to the Lord'. This praise is to be enriched by the accompaniment of the temple orchestra: the strumming of 'the harp', the blaring of 'trumpets' and the harsher powerful 'sound of the horn' are to combine to 'acclaim the King, the Lord'. However, as we shall see, that is not all.

'Let the sea and all within it, thunder; the world, and all its peoples. Let the rivers clap their hands and the hills ring out their joy at the presence of the Lord.'

There is a sense in which God's salvation is a further stage of his creative activity. And so at this point not only the temple orchestra, not only the whole 'world and all its peoples', but also the rest of creation – 'the sea and all [the strange monsters] within it', 'the rivers' and 'the hills' – are included in the call to praise the Lord. The sea is to 'thunder' its worship with all its mighty waves; still more picturesquely, the rivers are to 'clap their hands', while the hills are to stand tall and 'ring out their joy at the presence of the Lord'.

'For the Lord comes, he comes to rule the earth. He will rule the world with justice and the peoples with fairness.'

At this time of the year the Church's liturgy turns our thoughts to the future, to that day when Christ will return in glory as Judge of all humankind. Today's psalm catches the spirit of the liturgy, with its declaration that 'the Lord comes' and its brief explanation of the purpose of his coming – 'to rule the earth'. On that day, when his universal kingship is recognised by all, 'he will rule the world with justice'. When justice, divine justice, is done, all 'the peoples' will see the 'fairness' of his judgements: 'the arrogant and the evil-doers' (first reading) will suffer a fiery punishment, those who have been lazy (second reading) will be filled with shame; but those who have held on to their faith, who have endured despite all the difficulties of life (gospel), will sing and shout for joy – and the whole of nature will join them! Today's refrain is taken from this verse: 'The Lord comes to rule the peoples with fairness.'

LET US PRAY: *Lord, help us to realise that it is in the way we live our daily lives now that we are preparing for the Day of the Lord; when that great day comes may we be ready to sing a psalm of joy, an acclamation of praise to our King.*

Solemnity of Christ the King

Today's first reading (2 Samuel 5:1-3) tells how, some one thousand years before the birth of Christ, the people of Israel anointed David as their king.

The kingship of David was but a foreshadowing of the kingship of Jesus Christ our Lord; and it is in this kingdom of the Son whom he loves that the Father has prepared a place for us (Colossians 1:12-20).

Above Jesus' head as he hung on the cross there was an inscription, 'This is the King of the Jews'. It earned him the mockery of bystanders, but the confident trust of the 'good thief'; Jesus rewarded him in kingly fashion: 'today you will be with me in paradise' (Luke 23:35-43)

Today's psalm, Psalm 121, is not one of the enthronement psalms, as we might have expected. It is a psalm that focuses on Jerusalem, the capital city from which kings, beginning with David, ruled over the people in God's name.

Prayerful Ponderings

'I rejoiced when I heard them say: "Let us go to God's house."'
Psalm 121 stands as the third of the series of psalms known as
'Songs of Ascent'. Its opening words – just one word in Hebrew –
express the enthusiastic joy of pilgrims who have planned to 'go up'
to Jerusalem, site of the Temple which is revered as 'God's house'.
The implication is that when the idea was first mooted – 'Let us go
to God's house' – the psalmist already 'rejoiced'. But now that the
idea has become reality and the pilgrims have reached their
journey's end, the joy is all the greater; and that spirit of joy – so
appropriate to the great feast of Christ the King that we are
celebrating – seems to pervade the whole psalm. (The opening
sentence serves as the refrain to today's responsorial psalm.)

**'And now our feet are standing within your gates, O
Jerusalem. Jerusalem is built as a city strongly compact. It is
there that the tribes go up, the tribes of the Lord.'**
This verse marks the jubilant moment of arrival: the pilgrims are
actually 'standing within [the] gates' of Jerusalem. The very name
'Jerusalem' speaks of peace and security, for it 'is built as a city
strongly compact'. It is the city of God's people, where from time
immemorial the various 'tribes of the Lord' have gone up for the
annual festivals. It is the city that their great king David (first
reading) captured and made his capital. It is the city where through

earthly representatives God himself reigned and where his dwelling place, the Temple, was situated. (We remember that it is also the city where Jesus was sentenced to death because, his enemies alleged, he had claimed to be 'the King of the Jews'. As he was dying, there was one man at any rate who recognised him as a king, but a king unlike any other, a king whose kingdom would come into its own with his apparent defeat. And so the thief pleaded: 'Remember me when you come into your kingdom' [gospel].)

'For Israel's law it is, there to praise the Lord's name. There were set the thrones of judgement of the house of David.' The prime reason for the pilgrimage of the tribes to Jerusalem was not simply that they might meet each other, though no doubt that was a valuable bonus, but rather that, as 'Israel's law' made clear, they might 'praise the Lord's name' and give him thanks. Closely allied to the praise of God was the pursuit of justice. True worship of God cannot be divorced from justice among his children. 'The thrones of judgement' are the legal institutions, the equivalent of our courts of law, that had been set up by the Davidic kings. It would seem that on the occasion of the annual pilgrimages outstanding disputes would often be brought before the royal officials for a decision. If, as this psalm suggests, the pilgrimage to Jerusalem was a search for justice, it is no less true that today's feast might be described as a pilgrimage for justice, for the kingdom of the King we honour today is 'a kingdom of justice, love and peace'. There can be no genuine honouring of him in our worship unless there is a genuine pursuit of justice in our daily lives.

LET US PRAY: *Angels, saints and nations sing:*
'Praised be Jesus Christ, our King;
Lord of life, earth, sky and sea,
King of love on Calvary.'

OTHER FEASTS

that may be celebrated on a Sunday

The Ascension of the Lord

This festival has been celebrated with full solemnity since the fourth century as the final, glorious manifestation of our Lord's Easter exaltation, and Sunday by Sunday we profess our belief that 'he ascended into heaven'.

On this day, in each year of the three-year cycle, the first reading is always the same; it is the story of the ascension, as recounted by Luke in the Acts of the Apostles (1:1-11). Having instructed the apostles over a period of forty days, Jesus promises them the gift of the Holy Spirit, assures them that they are to be his witnesses 'to the ends of the earth' and then is lifted up until hidden from their sight by a cloud. As they gaze into the sky, an angel reminds them that until the day when Jesus returns, they have a job to do.

In the second reading (Hebrews 9:24-28; 10:19-23), which is optional for Year C, a comparison is drawn between the Jewish high priest, who annually, on the Day of Atonement, entered the Holy of Holies to win forgiveness for his people's sins, and Jesus, the great High Priest who, at his ascension, once and for all entered heaven itself and appeared 'in the actual presence of God on our behalf'. So he has made it possible for us to enter 'the sanctuary' of heaven.

The gospel (Luke 24:46-53) consists of Jesus' commissioning of his disciples to preach 'the forgiveness of sins ... to all the nations' and of his ascension when he 'was carried up to heaven'.

Psalm 46, from which today's responsorial psalm is drawn, was originally used as part of a solemn procession, perhaps one that brought the ark of the covenant, the sign of God's presence, into the Temple. There may even have been some kind of enthronement ceremony in recognition of God's everlasting kingship.

Prayerful Ponderings

'All peoples clap your hands, cry to God with shouts of joy! For the Lord, the Most High, we must fear, great king over all the earth.'

If in days gone by the people of Israel were encouraged to 'clap [their] hands' and 'cry … with shouts of joy' as they saw the ark of the covenant being borne in solemn procession to the Temple, how much more should we be encouraged to celebrate on this great day – even if our celebrations are a little more subdued – when we honour our Lord's being lifted up from this earth and borne into heaven itself. The Scripture readings we have heard today make it clear that everything possible must be done to ensure that one day 'all peoples' will join in our Ascension Day celebrations: with us they will honour a king who, though like to us in all things, is in fact 'the Lord, the Most High', a king whom 'we must fear', not because he is a tyrant but because he is so awesome and great. Such a one is by right 'great king over all the earth'.

'God goes up with shouts of joy; the Lord goes up with trumpet blast.'

It's hard to listen to these words, which make up the refrain of today's responsorial psalm, without sensing that something special is happening: they take us to the heart of the celebration. There is 'joy' in the air; besides the rhythmic clapping (see previous verse) and the shouts of delight, there is the sound of the 'trumpet', the ram's-horn trumpet (*shophar*) whose 'blast' marks important occasions, such as the New Year (Numbers 29:1) or the accession of a king (2 Kings 9:13) or, most significantly in this context, the occasion when David brought the ark to the city to make Jerusalem into God's abode (2 Samuel 6:15). And when the people proclaimed in this psalm: 'God goes up', 'the Lord goes up', was it part of a dramatised renewal (perhaps an annual renewal) of the first time the ark entered the Temple? And did they actually see the ark once more mounting towards the doors of the Temple where it would be enthroned? In any event today, through the liturgy, the ascension of the Lord is truly re-presented in our midst so that, with the eyes of faith, we see our Lord returning to the Father's house, and with joy we can cry out that the Lord does indeed go up.

'Sing praise for God, sing praise, sing praise to our king, sing praise. God is king of all the earth. Sing praise with all your skill.'

Again and again, again and again, the cry goes up: 'sing praise'. We have all heard a crowd giving vent to its feelings, not necessarily bad ones, by repeating some brief catch phrase over and over again. The very insistence of the cry to praise God in this psalm – 'sing praise for' him, 'sing praise to' him – suggests that it served a similar purpose, and it's easy to visualise the whole assembly chanting these words which sum up the sentiments of all. On this day a similar cry goes out from the Church: we are all invited to raise our voices in praise of the Lord, who has been raised to his heavenly throne as 'king of all the earth'.

'God is king over the nations; God reigns on his holy throne.' Though praise of God is important, even vital, yet by itself it is not enough. We cannot, dare not, forget that Jesus' final word to his disciples on the day of his ascension was in the form of their commissioning: their task was to be his witnesses, to take his message to the ends of the earth. On each subsequent Ascension Day the Church – and we are the Church – is called upon to renew its efforts to make known that 'God is king over the nations', whether they know it or not, that 'God reigns' over all the earth, and wants his reign to be acknowledged. More even than that, he wants all people to hear the good news that he 'has passed beyond our sight, not to abandon us but to be our hope' (Preface of the Mass for the Ascension).

LET US PRAY: *Lord our God, fill us with joy as we celebrate the ascension into heaven of our Lord Jesus Christ. Help us so to live our lives in this world that others will be brought to know and love him as King and God, and finally, where he, the Head, has already gone, may we, his members, most surely follow.*

The Body and Blood of Christ

Just as this solemnity in Year A focused on the bread of life and in Year B on the blood of the covenant, so in this year it seems to focus on the ministers of the Eucharist, and above all on Jesus as great High Priest.

The first reading (Genesis 14:18-20) tells how the priest-king Melchizedek met Abraham, as the latter was returning from a victory over a group of Canaanite kings. He brings an offering of bread and wine and shares with Abraham in an act of thanksgiving to 'God Most High'.

Psalm 109 is the obvious responsorial psalm for today: it mentions Melchizedek and speaks of him not only as king but also as priest. Moreover, the words of this psalm that make up the response – 'You are a priest for ever, a priest like Melchizedek of old' – apply perfectly to Jesus our great High Priest, who under the forms of bread and wine offers his supreme sacrifice in our midst for ever.

The gospel (Luke 9:11-17) tells how Jesus fed a multitude with a few loaves and fishes. It was his divine power that transformed this unlikely material into food for all, but 'he handed [the food] to his disciples to distribute among the crowd'. Similarly in the Eucharist, the transformation of the bread and wine is the work of Jesus through the ministry of ordained ministers, and the distribution of the sacrament is also in the hands of human ministers.

In the second reading (1 Corinthians 11:23-26) St Paul provides the first account we have of the institution of the Eucharist.

Prayerful Ponderings

'The Lord's revelation to my Master: "Sit on my right: I will put your foes beneath your feet." The Lord will send from Zion your sceptre of power: rule in the midst of all your foes.'
This psalm was used at the accession of a new king. Two messages, couched in language common to prophets, are delivered. The first is: 'The Lord's revelation to my Master' – the Lord, of course, being God himself. 'My Master' refers to the king who is addressed in this fashion because the prophet is his subject, one of his entourage. And the message itself is an invitation to the king to take his place on his throne on the 'right' hand of God, together with an assurance that God will subdue his foes, making them a royal footstool: 'Sit on my right: I will put your foes beneath your feet.' He will also give the new king the 'sceptre of power', the sign of his authority.

In the early Church the words 'sit on my right' – which Jesus himself referred to when on trial before the Sanhedrin (Matthew 26:64) – were seen to be fulfilled in the resurrection and ascension of Jesus. And, of course, every Sunday we profess our belief that Jesus 'is seated at the right hand of the Father'.

'A prince from the day of your birth on the holy mountains; from the womb before the daybreak I begot you.'
Though Psalm 109 is the psalm most frequently quoted in the

New Testament it is also one of the most difficult psalms to interpret, and no part of it is perhaps so difficult as this particular verse. However, its general sense, in the translation we have here, seems fairly clear: the king's coronation is, according to the popular view, the day on which he is reborn as son of God. His 'rebirth' takes place 'on the holy mountains' – where the plural, 'mountains', is the Hebrew way of stressing the lofty dignity of Mount Zion – where God dwells. He was divinely begotten 'before the daybreak', even before his coronation which ushers in a new dawn.

Of course, such language is excessive of any Davidic king but, as the letter to the Hebrews firmly asserts (chapter 5-7), Jesus Christ is the perfect fulfilment of this verse and the following one. He is indeed the only-begotten Son of God; his 'begetting' took place not on a high mountain but in the highest heavens, and it occurred from all eternity.

'The Lord has sworn an oath he will not change. "You are a priest for ever, a priest like Melchizedek of old."'

The second message for the king is in the form of an oath, an oath that is irrevocable. God has sworn: 'You are a priest for ever, a priest like Melchizedek of old.' Because, apart from his meeting with Abraham, nothing is known about Melchizedek's earlier or later history, it was popularly believed that he was an eternal priest, without beginning or end.

Once again, the language hardly makes sense when applied to a Davidic king, who is just as short-lived as any of his subjects. But when used of Jesus it makes perfect sense: he is indeed a priest for ever, he is a priest anointed by the Holy Spirit, he is a priest who offers a sacrifice under the appearances of bread and wine but infinitely more precious than that offered by Melchizedek (see first Eucharistic Prayer). Little wonder that this psalm has been described as the Messianic psalm above all others.

LET US PRAY: *Through baptism, Lord our God, we have become a priestly people, sharers in the unique priesthood of Jesus, your Son. Whether clergy or laity, may we ever deepen our appreciation of the Holy Eucharist, may we always treat the Blessed Sacrament with the greatest reverence and so give practical expression of our gratitude to Jesus Christ, our great High Priest, who lives and reigns with you and the Holy Spirit now and for ever.*

The Presentation
of the Lord (February 2)

Though for many centuries this feast was called the feast of the Purification of the Blessed Virgin Mary, its earlier title, one it had from its origin in the fourth century, was the Presentation of the Lord. The restoration of that title is a reminder that, like all Marian feasts, this one points to the indestructible link between Mary and her Son: it is through her that he is presented.

When Mary presents the Child, the prophecy of Malachi (3:1-4) is fulfilled, for he speaks of a day when 'the Lord will enter his Temple' – though he could never have believed that the Lord would arrive in the form of a babe-in-arms!

The second reading, taken from the letter to the Hebrews (2:14-18), underlines the reality of our Lord's humanity. Like any other first-born Jewish child, he had to be 'redeemed' forty days after his birth; like any one of us, he had to grow to maturity and, like any one of us, he was tried and tempted.

The gospel story (Luke 2:22-40) is something more than a bare account of the way in which Mary and Joseph complied with the Law. It serves as a formal announcement of Jesus' arrival in the Temple, his presentation to his people and, still more, his presentation to Jews and Gentiles alike as 'the salvation' of all humankind.

The second half of Psalm 23 is this Sunday's responsorial psalm. The earlier part speaks of the Lord as Maker and King of all creation and provides instruction on those who may worthily enter his presence; this part is applied to the arrival of the Lord himself in the Temple.

Prayerful Ponderings

'O gates, lift up your heads; grow higher, ancient doors. Let him enter, the king of glory!'

It seems likely that this psalm, especially this part of it, was composed as an accompaniment for a procession in which the ark of the covenant, the symbol of the Lord's presence, would be solemnly brought to the Temple, and there a festival celebrated in honour of his Kingship. In poetic language, the huge 'gates' which stand at the threshold of the Temple are commanded to 'lift up [their] heads' and the 'ancient doors' to 'grow higher', as though the entrance needs to be enlarged if it is to cope with the towering figure of the invisible Lord who is about to enter his palace, seated upon the ark as upon a throne. Nothing must be allowed to hinder the entry of 'the king of glory'.

'Who is the king of glory? The Lord, the mighty, the valiant, the Lord, the valiant in war.'

We can perhaps imagine the priests calling out, from inside the Temple, 'Who is [this] king of glory?', and back coming the response: 'The Lord, the mighty, the valiant'. We may find it difficult to feel sympathy for such a warlike God! However, the fact is that especially in earlier times the God of Israel was regarded as a mighty warrior: after all, he was more powerful than the pagan gods, and they, according to their adherents, had brought creation into being after the defeat of fierce enemies, and so, it was sometimes argued, Yahweh must have done the same; again, the people of Israel were confident that he had accompanied them, riding on the ark (which served as his chariot), when they went out to battle, so that they confidently styled him 'valiant in war'. Under the influence of the prophets these warlike titles came to take on a more general significance: they were ways of pointing to his greatness, his power, his holiness.

'O gates, lift high your heads; grow higher, ancient doors. Let him enter, the king of glor!.'

Once more the cry is raised that the gateway be enlarged to allow entry to 'the king of glory'. This time we might listen to it against the backcloth of today's feast. In the arms of Mary and Joseph, Jesus is coming to his Temple, coming to present himself as our Redeemer, 'the salvation … for all the nations', the one who restores us to God's friendship, the one who stands not only as 'the glory of … Israel' but also as 'a light … to the Gentiles' (hence, today's candle ceremony). And we are being invited to open the doors of our hearts to him, to rid ourselves of whatever might stand in the way of his coming, to enable him to become for us 'the king of glory'.

'Who is he, the king of glory? He, the Lord of armies, he is the king of glory.'

If the repeated query about the identity of 'the king of glory' again results in a warlike response, 'the Lord of armies', we have only to look at the tiny child in the arms of Mary and Joseph to realise that many faulty views about God stand in need of revision as a result of the incarnation. Ever since this child was born in the stable at Bethlehem, forty days ago, we have been gently reminded that our God is 'the king of glory' not only because he is all-powerful but also because he is so humble as to 'empty himself' and become 'completely like his brothers [and sisters]' (second reading). It is precisely through this self-emptying even to death on a cross that he has conquered in the only battle that matters, that against sin and Satan, and so set us free. Significantly, though the response to today's psalm is based on this verse, and its earlier counterpart, the answer it gives to 'Who is the king of glory?' makes no mention of military prowess; it states quite simply: 'It is the Lord.'

LET US PRAY: *Jesus, Son of God and Son of Mary, you are Lord. Come into our hearts, defeat all our spiritual enemies and be now and for ever our King of glory.*

Birth of John the Baptist
(June 24)

Four passages in Isaiah speak of a mysterious 'servant' of the Lord who suffers much but is the bearer of God's good news. Christian tradition has applied them to Jesus, but today's liturgy applies the second of them to John the Baptist, called as God's servant 'from my mother's womb', commissioned to bring Israel back to God and destined to be 'the light of the nations' (Isaiah 49:1-6).

The second reading (Acts 13:22-26), from Paul's sermon to the Jews at Antioch, speaks of John as the one who 'heralded' the coming of the Saviour and 'proclaimed … repentance', which is the precondition of conversion to the Lord.

The subjects of today's gospel (Luke 1:57-66, 80) are John's birth, the wonder surrounding his naming and the 'awe' which filled those present, leading them to wonder: 'What will this child turn out to be?'

Psalm 138, 'The Hound of Heaven' psalm, as it has been called, is a most appropriate psalm for today's feast, with its reference to God's knowledge and power which affect even those as yet unborn.

Prayerful Ponderings

'O Lord, you search me and you know me, you know my resting and my rising, you discern my purpose from afar. You mark when I walk or lie down, all my ways lie open to you.' This awesome and attractive psalm – unfortunately, only a few of its verses appear in the responsorial psalm – acclaims the unique character of God's knowledge, power and presence. John the Baptist, whose birth we celebrate today, must often have reflected on the wonderful relationship that existed between himself and God. Perhaps in the last dark days of his life, when he was being held captive in a subterranean dungeon by King Herod, he would have prayed this psalm, confident that God's discerning eye, which had always been upon him, was upon him still; that God's knowledge extended to even the most mundane of his everyday activities, such as 'my resting' and 'my rising', 'when I walk' and 'when I lie down'; that God's ability to read the human heart enabled him to 'discern [my] purpose from afar' – it was clear to God even before it was properly formed in the herald's own mind. However, this psalm is not just for great saints or for those who play an obviously crucial role in the Lord's plans; it is for everyone. Each of us can give thanks that our God is so close, that his loving knowledge of us is so all-embracing, that his understanding of us and our plans is so complete, that 'all [our] ways lie open' before him.

'For it was you who created my being, knit me together in my mother's womb.'

The words of the psalmist would have been particularly apt on the lips of John the Baptist, for John was born in answer to his parents' fervent prayers, even though both were old and Elizabeth 'was barren'. Not only John's birth and the events surrounding his circumcision, but even the fact of his conception must have caused the people to marvel and to wonder aloud: 'What will this child [so obviously due to God's intervention] turn out to be?' However, again we are invited to recognise that 'it was [the Lord] who created my being', it was he who 'knit me together in my mother's womb'. I am unique: not an accident but part of God's great design.

'I thank you for the wonder of my being, for the wonders of all your creation.'

Even the psalmist could appreciate the incredible craftsmanship that goes into the fashioning of a human being. And so the psalmist felt the need to thank God 'for the wonder of my being'; and that act of gratitude led on to a prayer of thanks for 'the wonders of all your creation'. Today we know so much more about the wonder of a human being – scientists have even mapped the human genome ('the language in which God created life', as President Clinton described it) – and yet perhaps there is still nothing so calculated to fill us with wonder as the sight of a newborn baby. People tend to express their astonishment as they take hold, for example, of the child's tiny fingers, and say with a sense of awe: 'Isn't he perfect! Isn't she wonderful!' Each of us is one of 'the wonders of [his] creation'; but through Jesus, whose coming was heralded by John, a still greater wonder has been worked in us: we have been re-created as sons and daughters of God.

'Already you knew my soul, my body held no secret from you when I was being fashioned in secret and moulded in the depths of the earth.'

This verse summarises what has gone before: it tells how we are known through and through, 'soul' and 'body', by the God who made us. Even when we were being 'moulded in the depths of the earth', a metaphor for the hiddenness of the womb, we 'held no secret from' the Lord. It is indeed a cause for wonder and gratitude that he who made the stars and the seas and the earth, was also involved in our prenatal development, fashioning us down to the tiniest detail so that we are, as the RSV translation puts it, 'intricately woven'. Again we need to remind ourselves on this day that God's creative work is involved in the fashioning not only of the great saints like John the Baptist but also of every single human being who is ever conceived.

LET US PRAY: *God our Father, on this day as we rejoice in the birth of John the Baptist, herald of our Saviour, we give thanks that through the saving work of Jesus Christ we, who are wondrously made, have become sharers in his divine Sonship.*

Saints Peter and Paul
(June 29)

Today's first reading (Acts 12:1-11) records how, when Peter was imprisoned, 'the Church prayed to God for him unremittingly' and how he was miraculously released.

Paul is able to make the proud boast: 'I have fought the good fight to the end… I have kept the faith'. But he acknowledges that it was the Lord who 'rescued [him] from the lion's mouth' and prays that glory may be given to the Lord for ever (2 Timothy 4:6-8, 17-18).

The gospel (Matthew 16:13-19) is the account of Peter's recognition of Jesus as 'the Christ' and Jesus' designation of Peter as the rock on which 'I will build my Church'.

Today's psalm is taken from the first part of a song of thanksgiving (Psalm 33) which praises God, in particular for the psalmist's own experience of deliverance.

Prayerful Ponderings

'I will bless the Lord at all times, his praise always on my lips: in the Lord my soul shall make its boast. The humble shall hear and be glad.'

The psalmist boldly proclaims his resolve to 'bless the Lord at all times', to have 'his praise always on my lips', to ensure that only 'in the Lord my soul shall make its boast'. Moreover, it is his belief that 'the humble', those who are attuned to the Lord's ways, will rejoice with him and 'be glad' when they 'hear' what the Lord has done for him. Such sentiments would surely be dear to the heart of St Paul for he was a truly grateful man. In the first of his letters which has come down to us, he urges his friends in Thessalonica to give thanks to the Lord 'in all circumstances' (1 Thessalonians 5:18). The implication is that that is what he did himself; indeed, the notion of thanksgiving occurs so many times in his subsequent correspondence that it might well be described as one of his theme songs.

'Glorify the Lord with me. Together let us praise his name. I sought the Lord and he answered me; from all my terrors he set me free.'

Both Peter and Paul could look back on situations where they had been set free 'from all [their] terrors' by the intervention of the Lord. Peter was 'sprung' from his prison cell (first reading) despite the elaborate precautions taken against his escape, and Paul recalls how he was 'rescued from the lion's mouth' (though we have no means of knowing what – or who – the lion may have been). So each might have urged the other to 'glorify the Lord with me. Together let us praise his name.' However, on this feast day we are all being invited to join them in glorifying, praising and thanking the Lord for all that he has done through these two great apostles. Once they had discovered, or, better been discovered by, Christ and recognised him as Lord, they sought him and his will all the rest of their days. Many times they had to face 'terrors' – in the end they had to face the threat of death itself for his sake and that of the gospel – and still they remained confident that 'he [would] set [them] free'.

'Look towards him and be radiant; let your faces not be abashed. This poor man called; the Lord heard him and rescued him from all his distress.'
No one can 'look towards [the Lord]' with faith and trust without becoming 'radiant', without catching a certain likeness to him; it is what Paul seems to be referring to when he says that 'all of us, with unveiled face, seeing the glory of the Lord … are being transformed into the same image from one degree of glory to another' (2 Corinthians 3:18). The apostles would have us know that despite our weakness we need not 'be abashed'; like many a 'poor man [who has] called [on the Lord]', we can be sure that the Lord will hear and will rescue us from 'all [our] distress'.

'The angel of the Lord is encamped around those who revere him, to rescue them. Taste and see that the Lord is good. He is happy who seeks refuge in him.'

Often in the Hebrew Scriptures the expression 'the angel of the Lord' is used of God himself, particularly when he intervenes in human affairs. His presence is like a protective army 'encamped around those who revere him'; he is ready 'to rescue them', whatever their plight. The psalmist's advice is straightforward: 'Taste and see that the Lord is good'; it is as though he were saying: I've given my testimony, now it's up to you to sample the Lord for yourself; then you'll discover that you are safe in his hands. That discovery was certainly made by the two saints we honour today: they are foundations on which the Church rests. Finally, it's worth noting that the advice to 'taste and see that the Lord is good' is applied in the New Testament to Christians who have newly received the sacrament of baptism (1 Peter 2:3), while among the early Fathers of the Church it is also used in reference to the Holy Eucharist.

LET US PRAY: *We pray, Lord our God, that the Church throughout the world may be inspired by the noble apostles Peter and Paul and that, like them, all Christians may taste and experience your unbounded goodness and all-powerful protection.*

The Transfiguration of the Lord (August 6)

Written when the Jews were reeling under Syrian persecution, the first reading, from the book of Daniel (7:9-10, 13-14), offers encouragement by reminding them, on the one hand, of God in the guise of 'one of great age' ablaze with glory, and, on the other, of God's representative, 'one like a son of man' on whom 'sovereignty, glory and kingship' are conferred and who is worshipped by all the nations. It is that representative who is at the centre of today's feast.

Peter, to whom the second reading (2 Peter 1:16-19) is attributed, recalls that what Christians believe are not 'cleverly invented myths' but events of which he, and others, were witnesses. And so, he claims, 'we were with him on the holy mountain' (of transfiguration).

The gospel for this feast (Luke 9:28-36) is always an account of the transfiguration, but, depending upon which year it is within the three-yearly cycle, the passage is taken either from the Gospel of Matthew or that of Mark or that of Luke.

Psalm 96 is one of the 'enthronement psalms', praising God for his universal reign, but also emphasising the fact that he has saved his people.

Prayerful Ponderings

'The Lord is king, let earth rejoice, let all the coastlands be glad. Cloud and darkness are his raiment; his throne justice and right.'

Much of the imagery in this psalm seems to have been borrowed from the religions of surrounding nations which commonly depicted their 'god' achieving kingship by defeating lesser 'gods' in battle. The psalm begins with a simple but powerful statement – 'the Lord is king' – which will be elaborated in the rest of the song, though in fact only a few verses appear in today's responsorial psalm. To begin with, his kingship is an invitation to the whole 'earth' to 'rejoice' and 'all the coastlands' to 'be glad'. Mysterious 'cloud and darkness' both conceal him and serve as signs of his presence, just as they had been on Mount Sinai (and of course on the mount of transfiguration Jesus was overshadowed by a bright cloud [see gospel]); they are even looked upon as 'his raiment', his royal robes, while the 'throne' on which he is seated has as its bases 'justice and right'. A royal throne has always stood as a symbol of kingship, and the Lord's throne could not be more firmly based, for it rests on the twin qualities of justice and right. Justice embraces all those divine actions and decisions which lead to righteousness, to a way of life that is rich and fulfilling.

'The mountains melt like wax before the Lord of all the earth. The skies proclaim his justice; all peoples see his glory.'

Next, the very 'mountains', despite their apparently immovable solidity, are compared to a piece of 'wax' melting away in the overwhelming presence of 'the [mighty] Lord of all the earth'. Meanwhile 'the skies' take up the proclamation of 'his justice': he is a judge who can be depended upon always to act with fairness and impartiality. And finally there is the promise that 'all peoples' will 'see his glory'. On the mount of transfiguration the apostles saw their Master so utterly open to the Father that the Father's glory shone through his person and his very garments, while the voice of the Father proclaimed him as his beloved Son. In the liturgy of today's feast we too are granted a vision of our Lord in glory, one truly like us – 'one like a son of man' as Daniel describes him (first reading) – but at the same time one on whom has been conferred 'sovereignty, glory and kinship'.

'For you indeed are the Lord, most high above all the earth, exalted far above all spirits.'

The refrain of today's psalm is made up of a phrase from this verse of the psalm – 'most high above all the earth' – prefaced by the exclamation 'the Lord is king'. To hail Jesus as Lord is already to hail him as king, is already to acknowledge that he is 'exalted far above' not only all earth and all people but also 'above all spirits'. On this day we are filled with wonder for we see how the Jesus who walked the streets of Palestine has been revealed as the glorious image of the Father and as supreme Lord of all creation. He stands for us 'as a lamp for lighting a way through the dark until the dawn [of our resurrection] comes and the morning star rises' (second reading).

LET US PRAY: *We bow down in wonder before you, Lord Jesus, truly the only Son of the Father but also our brother, like to us in all things but sin. As you have shared our common lot of suffering and even of death, so may we one day share in full measure in your heavenly glory.*

The Assumption of the Blessed Virgin Mary (August 15)

The first reading (Revelation 11:19; 12:1-6, 10) comes from a type of literature (apocalyptic) which aimed to give reassurance in time of persecution. 'The woman' it speaks of refers in the first place to the Church: she will survive the Roman offensive that has been mounted against her. But it is also applied to Mary who is mother of the Messiah, mother of the Church and first and most perfect Christian disciple.

Through Christ, the second Adam, has come hope of resurrection from the dead; he is the first to rise in glory. Today's feast teaches us that Mary was the second to share his triumph to the full and is a pledge for us of the resurrection that awaits us beyond death (1 Corinthians 15:20-26).

The gospel for today (Luke 1:39-56) tells the delightful story of the Visitation; it is a story which revolves around the woman who is to bring us our Messiah. Through him will come salvation and the promise of resurrection from the dead. Today we rejoice in the belief that the promise has already been fulfilled – in the Assumption of Mary, body and soul, into the glory of heaven.

Psalm 44, which provides the two verses which make up today's responsorial psalm, was originally a wedding song for a Davidic king but later came to be recognised as Messianic, as achieving its fulfilment in the Davidic king, Jesus Christ; the 'queen' who is shown standing beside him is applied in today's feast to Mary taken up into the heavenly palace of her Son.

Prayerful Ponderings

'The daughters of kings are among your loved ones. On your right stands the queen in gold of Ophir.'

A royal wedding was always an important event and this psalm reflects the magnificence of such an occasion. Extravagant praise is lavished on the king: 'your ladies of honour' (the translation which the RSV prefers to 'your loved ones') are members of royal families, they are in fact 'the daughters of kings'. But 'on [his] right' in the place of honour – and this is the climax of the passage – 'stands the queen' herself. She is dressed in beautiful robes interwoven with glistening 'gold of Ophir', the most costly gold that could be found. All eyes are on the bride: 'on your right stands the queen, in garments of gold' is the constantly repeated refrain of today's Mass. We too are meant to fix our eyes upon her, seeing in her the completed model, so to say, of what we all shall be one day, provided only that we are faithful to the Lord. The reference to her vesture of gold might remind us of the many blessings with which God has clothed her to prepare her to be a worthy mother of his Son. However, it is because she responded so wholeheartedly with those graces that she is the symbol of the Church. Moreover, she knows how indebted she is: for ever she will acknowledge (see the Magnificat in today's Mass) 'the Almighty has done great things for me. Holy is his name'

'Listen, O daughter, give ear to my words: forget your own people and your father's house.'

The king begs his new queen ('daughter' he calls her) to 'give ear to my words', in the double sense of listening carefully to them and acting upon them; in the gospel Mary is portrayed precisely as someone who 'pondered' in her heart all that happened to her, all that was said to her, and at the same time was always ready to respond as the humble handmaid of the Lord. According to this verse, the queen is also called upon to 'forget [her] own people and [her] father's house'. In its original context this rather extreme advice perhaps meant little more than that she must give up her own home and family and enter the king's abode, become part of his family and be totally devoted to him. (It has been suggested that she was a foreign princess and so would literally have had to leave her home and family behind.) Mary too, in becoming mother of the Saviour, had to set out on a new way of life: everything must have been so different for her, perhaps she had to abandon her plans to marry Joseph, certainly she had to be prepared to follow her Son wherever it might take her – even to the summit of Calvary.

'So will the king desire your beauty: he is your lord, pay homage to him.'

'The king' of the psalm may well have been overwhelmed by the physical 'beauty' of his young wife, but it was above all the spiritual beauty of Mary that was so pleasing to the Lord. The queen of the psalm was also reminded that her husband was her 'lord' and that therefore she must 'pay homage to him' – in the days of the psalmist a wife's submission to her husband was taken for granted – but Mary had no need to be reminded of her duties to the Lord; her whole life was shot through with praise, she desired only to 'magnify the Lord' in all that she did. As the first and perfect Christian she gladly paid him homage.

'They are escorted amid gladness and joy; they pass within the palace of the king.'

The mysterious 'they' of this verse are the queen's bridesmaids. They have known her perhaps from childhood and it is a moment of immense 'gladness and joy' when the solemn moment arrives for the bridal pair and their attendants to solemnly enter 'the palace of the king'. A new life has begun. On this day we celebrate Mary's solemn entry into the palace of the King of kings; but she does not go alone. She is the first of all those who will share her triumph, who, like her, will be body and soul in the glory of heaven.

LET US PRAY: *We beg you, Mary our Mother, to pray for us that, following your example, we may serve the Lord faithfully all our days and at the last enjoy eternal gladness and joy in the palace of Jesus, our Lord and King.*

The Triumph
of the Cross (September 14)

Today's first reading (Numbers 21:4-9) takes us back to Israel's days in the desert. There, because of their rebellion against God, 'fiery serpents' were let loose upon them. Many died. Moses was instructed to erect a bronze serpent on a pole; whoever looked upon it would live.

The gospel (John 3:13-17) draws a striking parallel between the raising up of the serpent in the desert and the lifting up of Jesus on the cross 'so that everyone who believes in him … may have eternal life'.

The second reading is the beautiful hymn from St Paul's letter to the Philippians (2:6-11) which records how Jesus, putting aside his glory, humbled himself to the point of death – even death on a cross. By his obedience our rebellions are healed.

The verses which make up today's responsorial psalm are taken from the lengthy Psalm 77 (no less than 70-odd verses long!), one of three great historical psalms which tell the story of God's dealing with his people, especially at the Exodus, during their desert journeyings and on their arrival in the Promised Land.

Prayerful Ponderings

'Never forget the deeds of the Lord.'
A nation forgetful of its own past has been likened to a person
suffering from loss of memory. The people of Israel were never in
danger of such amnesia because biblical faith is a 'remembering'
faith, a faith rooted in history (Guttiérez), a faith which will 'never'
allow the people to 'forget the deeds of the Lord'. Though these
words are not an exact excerpt from the psalm, they do in fact serve
as a perfect summary of it, for time and again throughout the song
the importance of remembering is underlined.

**'Give heed, my people, to my teaching; turn your ear to the
words of my mouth. I will open my mouth in a parable and
reveal hidden lessons of the past.'**
The opening words of the psalm are usually described as 'wisdom
instruction'. The 'wise men' or sages in the ancient Near East were
renowned for their discernment and teaching ability. They would
expect the 'people' to 'give heed… to my teaching', would call
upon them to 'turn [their] ear to the words of my mouth' and
would promise to speak to them 'in a parable' (or wise saying) and
in particular to 'reveal [to them] hidden lessons of the past'. On this
day we are invited to be wise enough to listen carefully to the
history of our ancestors in faith, for we too have much to learn
from it.

'When he slew them then they would seek him, return and seek him in earnest. They would remember that God was their rock, God the Most High their redeemer.'

After the introductory verse, we are led at once to a later section of the psalm which is concerned with the desert wanderings of the people of Israel. Despite all that God had done in rescuing them from slavery in Egypt, they had chosen to murmur against him (first reading), to rebel against him. Then, when he took action against them ('he slew them' is the way the psalmist describes it), 'they would seek him' again, they would 'return and seek him in earnest'. They 'would remember'- the very thing that we are all asked to do today – remember that he is 'their rock', their abiding support, that he is 'God the Most High', that he is 'their redeemer'.

'But the words they spoke were mere flattery; they lied to him with their lips. For their hearts were not truly with him; they were not faithful to his covenant.'

However, their display of repentance, apparently so earnest, was completely deceptive, for 'the words they spoke were mere flattery'. The situation is not unlike that addressed by the prophet Hosea when he told the people, in God's name: 'Your love is like a morning cloud, like the dew that goes away early' (6:4). All that they had said 'with their lips' were so many lies because there was no real repentance, 'their hearts were not truly with him' and that was shown by the way they lived their lives: quite simply, 'they were not faithful to his covenant'. However, on this feast day especially, we dare not forget that we too, despite all our promises and good intentions, continue to fail the Lord in so many ways. As St James reminds us, we still have to learn how to be 'doers of the word and not merely hearers who deceive themselves' (James 1:22).

'Yet he who is full of compassion forgave their sin and spared them. So often he held back his anger when he might have stirred up his rage.'

Thankfully, our God does not treat us as we deserve, for he 'is full of compassion'; just as he 'forgave their sin' and 'spared' his people, so he continues to spare us and forgive us. The psalmist remarks – it sounds almost in unbelief – that 'so often he held back his anger' when what might have been expected was that he would 'have stirred up his rage'. Still more do we have reason to marvel at the long-suffering compassion of our God; over and over again we have to confess our failures and sins – that's the way we begin almost every Mass – and yet we have confidence to believe that he will have mercy and spare us. That lonely figure, hoisted up on the cross of Calvary, is the reason for our hope. If he is prepared to lower himself to this level (see second reading) in order to save us, then we can indeed look up to him in faith and be confident that we shall be healed, no matter how terrible our unfaithfulness..

LET US PRAY: *Lord, may we heed the wise words of the psalmist; may we never forget your mighty deeds and never lose sight of your compassion and your readiness to save; may we recognise the cross of Calvary as the symbol not of tragedy but of glorious triumph.*

All Saints
(November 1)

The first reading (Revelation 7:2-4, 9-14) speaks of the countless host of men and women from every time and place who now see the face of God.

John (1 John 3:1-3) gives us the incredible news that already we are 'God's children' but that we are destined to 'be [still more] like him because we shall see him as he really is'.

In the Beatitudes (Matthew 5:1-12), Jesus speaks of the happiness, the blessedness, of those who are poor, who are gentle, etc. By earthly standards such people may seem to be losers but in fact they are the children of God, destined for 'the kingdom of heaven'.

Psalm 23 is a hymn in honour of the Kingship of the Lord; the verses used for the responsorial psalm are, appropriately for today's feast, in the form of an entrance liturgy, announcing the kind of people who will be allowed into the presence of God.

Prayerful Ponderings

'The Lord's is the earth and its fullness, the world and all its
peoples. It is he who set it on the seas; on the waters he made it
firm.'

This opening verse sets the scene for all that follows; we are introduced
to the Lord, to whom belongs the whole of nature, 'the earth and its
fullness', and the whole of humanity , 'the world and all its peoples'. All
belongs to him because he is the great creator. In the psalmist's day the
world was pictured as being surrounded on all sides by a watery waste,
and God himself as conquering the fierce waters, so that he is able to 'set
[the world] on the seas', to fix it on stout pillars so that it will remain
'firm' and secure amidst 'the [heaving, chaotic] waters' of the deep. This
is the God whom the pilgrims are now about to approach.

'Who shall climb the mountain of the Lord? Who shall stand
in his holy place?'

In the light of the poet's description of the mighty creative work
of God, an obvious question arises: Who would ever be worthy to
'stand in his holy place', to enter into the presence of a God such
as this? Of course the psalmist is thinking only in terms of the
Temple in Jerusalem: before pilgrims ascend 'the mountain' on
which the Temple is built, they wonder who will be able to 'climb
the mountain of the Lord' with good conscience. However, on this
feast day, the question is a more extraordinary one: Who dare think

of entry into God's temple in heaven, entry into the very presence of God himself?

'The man with clean hands and pure heart, who desires not worthless things. He shall receive blessings from the Lord and reward from the God who saves him.'

The psalmist tries to answer the first question raised by the previous verse, as to who might worthily make his or her way into the Temple. But the answer, provided in all probability by one of the temple personnel, may also be accommodated to the second question, which is concerned with those worthy of entrance into heaven itself. It is those who have 'clean hands and pure hearts' because they do no wrong to others and above all because they have set their hearts on the Lord rather than on any 'worthless things'. They are the people spoken of in the first reading: who have been faithful to God through every trial, who 'have washed their robes white ... in the blood of the Lamb'. They are the beatitude people spoken of in the gospel: those who have known their need of God, those who are gentle, those who hunger and thirst for what is right, those who are merciful, those who are peacemakers, those single-minded people who are described by Jesus as 'the pure of heart' and the children of God. Even on earth they bore the likeness of the Lord because of the way they lived their lives and today we celebrate the fact that they are still more wonderfully 'like him' because now they 'see him as he really is' (second reading). The promise has indeed been fulfilled: they have received 'blessings from the Lord' and a 'reward' beyond their wildest dreams. But they will always remember that their eternal reward is due not to themselves but rather to 'the God who saves them'.

'Such are the men who seek him, seek the face of the God of Jacob.'

This verse is also the refrain for today's responsorial psalm. In its original setting it was simply a confirmation that those approaching the Temple were worthy to enter. But today we might use it in the form of a prayer: we are the people 'who seek [you]', we are the people who 'seek [your] face'. The psalm may suggest that those worthy of God's presence are completely perfect, and maybe the readings seem to confirm that same impression. However, among the saints whom we honour today are people whom we have known and loved; many of them are 'ordinary' people, with their weaknesses and defects and sinfulness. They have striven hard but ultimately they are in heaven because of the mercy of God. And the same will be true of ourselves. Despite all our inadequacies – and worse – our hearts are set on God; we do long to see his face and we do trust that he will one day enable us to join that countless throng gathered before his throne.

LET US PRAY: *Great and mighty God, we praise you on this day for all the wonders of your creation but still more for the wonders of spiritual re-creation which you have worked in your saints. We too seek your face; may there come a time when we shall be numbered among those who are honoured on the feast of All Saints.*

The Dedication of the Lateran Basilica (November 9)

Today's feast commemorates the dedication of the Mother Church of Christendom: St John Lateran is the Pope's own cathedral church. The first reading (Ezekiel 47:1-2, 8-9, 12), with its account of a stream of water flowing from the Temple and bringing life wherever it flows, is meant to remind us of the blessings that God bestows upon people everywhere through his Church.

Paul (1 Corinthians 3:9-11, 16-17) describes the Church as a living temple; it is a sacred temple, indwelt by the Holy Spirit and with Jesus Christ as its sole foundation.

In response to those who attack him for his cleansing of the Temple in Jerusalem, Jesus speaks of himself as a sanctuary which, three days after its destruction, he will raise up (John 2:13-22).

Psalm 45 is the first of a group of psalms which hymn the glory of Jerusalem, the Lord's own city. It is because his Temple is founded there that it will stand firm against every assault. Verses from this 'song of Sion' feature in today's Mass: Jesus dwells for ever in his Church.

Prayerful Ponderings

'God is for us a refuge and strength, a helper close at hand, in time of distress: so we shall not fear though the earth should rock, though the mountains fall into the depths of the sea.'

A psalm could hardly begin with a more powerful confession of trust in God. He is saluted as 'a refuge and strength', one who defends us and empowers us in our difficulties, and as one always ready to help us for he is 'a helper close at hand, in time of distress'. In response to such statements of confidence, 'we', the people gathered in worship, declare that 'we shall not fear', not even if those apparently most stable elements, the earth and the mountains, should come to grief. We shall not fear 'though the earth [itself] should rock' and the burly mountains totter and 'fall into the depths of the sea'. St John Lateran's is the Pope's own church, and, as an inscription at its east end explains, it is 'Mother and Head of All Churches … throughout the world'. And so on this feast day we are meant to give thanks for the world-wide unity of the Church, a unity which centres around the Holy Father. It was after proclaiming Peter as 'the rock on which I will build my Church' that Jesus promised that, despite enemies from without and scandals from within, his Church would stand firm for ever, and that not even 'the gates of hell' would prevail against it (Matthew 16:18).

'The waters of a river give joy to God's city, the holy place where the Most High dwells. God is within, it cannot be shaken; God will help it at the dawning of the day.'

The mysterious reference to 'the waters of a river' perhaps reflects an ancient belief that the home of the gods is surrounded by a stream which serves as a life-giving source. There is a similar allusion in the description of the river flowing out of the garden of Eden in Genesis 2:10-12, as well as in the account of the life-giving stream in today's first reading. Jerusalem is 'God's city' and 'the holy place where the Most High dwells'; it is his presence that ensures its security against all its enemies; 'at the dawning of the day', when enemies often decide to mount an attack, he will be there to help and protect it. On this feast day we remember with gratitude that the survival of the Church throughout the ages − 'it cannot be shaken' to destruction − is ultimately due to the fact that it stands in the world as the city of God; it is he who dwells in its midst, it is he who ensures that while it is always in need of reform it is also a source of health and holiness for the whole human race.

'The Lord of hosts is with us: the God of Jacob is our stronghold. Come consider the works of the Lord, the redoubtable deeds he has done on the earth.'

The cry 'the Lord of hosts is with us' is a confident declaration that God with his heavenly army of angels is there to defend us. It is not anything we can do that gives us our security, but the fact that he 'is our stronghold'. We have only to consider 'the works of the Lord', says the psalmist, only to reflect on 'the redoubtable deeds he has done on the earth' and, it seems to be implied, we shall have no reason to fear. No doubt the psalmist is thinking of all that God has done for his people throughout their history, beginning with the Exodus from Egypt. But today when we profess our trust in the God who dwells within his Church, we recall 'the redoubtable deeds' that Jesus has accomplished from his birth in the stable of Bethlehem, to his public ministry, to his death and glorious resurrection, to his sending of the Holy Spirit so that the Church might spring to life as his Mystical Body. We know that he will be with us 'always, even to the end of the age' (Matthew 28:20).

LET US PRAY: *On this day, we give thanks that the risen Lord is the new Temple in which God is worshipped in spirit and in truth, that we have been built up as living stones in that Temple and that, bound together in unity under Peter's successor, we are confident that the Lord of hosts will be with us throughout the ages.*

The Immaculate Conception of the Blessed Virgin Mary (December 8)

From the first reading of this Mass (Genesis 3:9-15, 20) it becomes clear that today's feast links Mary intimately with her Son; it is her role in salvation history that is stressed. The promise, following upon the 'fall' of our first parents, that there would be a woman whose child is destined to crush the head of the 'serpent' already hints at the work accomplished by the Mother and her Child, Mary and Jesus.

The redemptive work of Christ is beautifully outlined in the second reading (Ephesians 1:3-6, 11-12); the richest beneficiary of that work is Mary, whom the Father 'chose in Christ' from all eternity that she might be 'holy and spotless' and so a worthy mother for his Son.

The gospel account of the Annunciation (Luke 1:26-38) shows Mary being greeted by the angel as 'full of grace', a fullness which she has known from the first instant of her existence.

Psalm 97 is an Enthronement Psalm, praising the Lord as King. The verses chosen for today's great feast rejoice in the saving work of God and, by implication, in the part that Mary played in that work as mother of the Saviour.

Prayerful Ponderings

'Sing a new song to the Lord for he has worked wonders. His right hand and his holy arm have brought salvation.'

The first sentence, which is the beginning of Psalm 97 and also the refrain of today's responsorial psalm, is a call to 'sing a new song to the Lord'. The song is new not because it is newly composed but because it is an invitation to consider anew the saving work of the Lord, and on this day especially it is a call to praise God for the unique place he has allotted in his plans to the young maiden, Mary of Nazareth. It is a call addressed to all the redeemed, who have benefited so magnificently from the 'wonders' that 'he has worked' through Jesus (see second reading), wonders which are greater even than those worked at the Exodus. Like a warrior, whose hands and arms overcome the foe, Jesus is pictured as overcoming our deadliest foes, sin and death, by 'his right hand and his holy arm'. However, we cannot forget that his hands were nailed to a wooden beam, his arms stretched on a cross in order to achieve our 'salvation'.

'The Lord has made known his salvation; has shown his justice to the nations. He has remembered his truth and love for the house of Israel.'

The first, as well as the supreme, beneficiary of the Lord's saving work is Mary. In her we see what 'salvation' means: it is not simply forgiveness of sin or even preservation from sin (as the title of Immaculate Conception might suggest) but rather something gloriously joyful and positive. Mary is 'highly favoured'; from the first moment of her existence she is so intimately united with God that there is no room for sin in her life, so completely his that she is the embodiment of all we mean by 'salvation' (see the gospel). And so, in her, God 'has shown his justice [his plan to draw all men and women into his friendship] to [all] the nations'; in her he has shown forth his steadfast 'love' for his people, 'the house of Israel': he has been true to all his promises of old.

'All the ends of the earth have seen the salvation of our God.'
The story of the garden of Eden tells of human rebellion against God; abusing the wonderful gift of freedom, human creatures make wrong choices and so separate themselves from God and from one another (see first reading). And yet from the beginning God had already planned to come to our rescue so that we could become 'his adopted sons [and daughters]'. Through Jesus, whose very name means 'salvation', the divine plan is revealed to 'the ends of the earth', and, at the heart of that plan, God has shown his immense respect for human freedom: the coming of the Saviour was made dependent upon the free consent of Mary (see the gospel).

'Shout to the Lord, all the earth, ring ouy your joy'.
The responsorial psalm ends in much the same way as it began with a summons to praise the Lord, though this time we are invited to 'shout to the Lord' and to 'ring out [our] joy', and the summons goes out to 'all the earth'. Today is indeed a celebration, a celebration of God's merciful goodness, his matchless love for his

creatures, but also a celebration of a woman, one of us, who in view of the motherhood that was to be hers was conceived immaculate (God's favour was always with her) and who when the time came was ready to give her wholehearted consent. And so it was that the Word was made flesh and dwelt among us. Alleluia!

LET US PRAY: *Heavenly Father, you chose Mary from all women to be our advocate with you and our pattern of holiness. Following her example, may we always be ready to say a wholehearted Yes to your designs so that, like Mary, we may bring Christ to others and so continue your saving work in the world.*

APPENDIX

Psalms	Sundays/Feasts
1:1-4,6	6th Ordinary (C)
4:2,4,7,9	3rd Easter (B)
8:4-9	Trinity Sunday (C)
14:1-5	22nd Ordinary (B)
	16th Ordinary (C)
15:1-2,5,7-11	3rd Easter (A)
	13th Ordinary (C)
15:1,5,8-11	33rd Ordinary (B)
16:1,5-6,8,15	32nd Ordinary (C)
17:2-4,47,51	30th Ordinary (A)
	31st Ordinary (B)
18:8-11	3rd Lent (B)
18:8-10,15	3rd Ordinary (C)
18:8-10,12-14	26th Ordinary (B)
21:8-9,17-20,23-24	Passion Sunday (A,B,C)
21:26-28,30-32	5th Easter (B)
22	4th Lent (A)
	4th Easter (A)
	28th Ordinary (A)
	16th Ordinary (B)
22:1-3,5-6	Christ the King (A)
23:1-6	4th Advent (A)
	All Saints
23:7-10	The Presentation of the Lord
24:4-5,8-9,10,14	1st Advent (C)
24:4-9	26th Ordinary (A)
	1st Lent (B)
	3rd Ordinary (B)
26:1,4,13-14	3rd Ordinary (A)
26:1,4,7-8	7th Easter (A)
26:1,7-9,13-14	2nd Lent (C)
28:1-4,9-10	Baptism of the Lord (A)
29:2,4-6,11-13	13th Ordinary (B)
	3rd Easter (C)
	10th Ordinary (C)

30:2-4,17,25	9th Ordinary (A)
31:1-2,5,7, 11	6th Ordinary (B)
	11th Ordinary (C)
32:1-2,4-5,18-19	5th Easter (A)
32:1,12,18-20	19th Ordinary (C)
32:2-3,7,17-19	30th Ordinary (C)
32:4-5,18-20,22	2nd Lent (A)
	29th Ordinary (B)
32:4-6,9,18-20,22	Most Holy Trinity (B)
33:2-7,9	4th Lent (C)
33:2-9	19th Ordinary (B)
	SS Peter and Paul, Apostles
33:2-3,10-15,9	20th Ordinary (B)
33:2-3,16-23	21st Ordinary (B)
39:2,4,7-10	2nd Ordinary (A,B)
39:2-4,14,18	20th Ordinary (C)
40:2-5,13-14	7th Ordinary (B)
44:10-12,16	The Assumption
45:2-3,5-6,8-9	Dedication of Lateran Basilica
46:2-3,6-9	Ascension of the Lord (A,B,C)
49:1-8,12-15	10th Ordinary (A)
50:3-4,12-15	5th Lent (B)
50:3-4,12-13,17,19 + Luke15:18	24th Ordinary (C)
50:3-6,12-14,17	1st Lent (A)
53:3-6,8	25th Ordinary (B)
61:2-3,6-9	8th Ordinary (A)
62:2-8	32nd Ordinary (A)
62:2-6,8-9	22nd Ordinary (A)
	12th Ordinary (C)
64:10-14	15th Ordinary (A)
65:1-7,16,20	6th Easter (A)
	14th Ordinary (C)
66:2-3,5,6,8	Mary, Mother of God (A,B,C)
	20th Ordinary (A)
66:2-3,4-8	6th Easter (C)
67:4-7,10-11	22nd Ordinary (C)
68:8-10,14,17,33-35	12th Ordinary (A)

68:14,17,30-31,33-34,36-37	15th Ordinary (C)
70:1-6,15,17	4th Ordinary (C)
	Birth of John the Baptist
71:1-2,7-8,12-12,17	2nd Advent (A)
71:1-2,7-8,10-13	Epiphany (A, B, C)
71:1-2,7,34-38	Triumph of the Cross
77:3-4,23-25,54	18th Ordinary (B)
79:2-3,15-16,18-19	1st Advent (B)
	4th Advent (C)
79:9,12-16,19-20	27th Ordinary (A)
80:2-8,10-11	9th Ordinary (B)
83:2-3,5-6,9-10	Holy Family (C)
84:9-12	2nd Advent (B)
84:9-14	19th Ordinary (A)
	15th Ordinary (B)
85:5-6,9-10,15-16	16th Ordinary (A)
88:2-3,16-19	13th Ordinary (A)
88:2-5,27,29	4th Advent (B)
89:1,3-6,12-14	18th Ordinary (C)
	23rd Ordinary (C)
89:12-17	28th Ordinary (B)
90:1-2,10-15	1st Lent (C)
91:2-3,13-16	11th Ordinary (B)
	8th Ordinary (C)
92:1-2,5	Christ the King (B)
94:1-2,6-9	3rd Lent (A)
	23rd Ordinary (A)
	4th Ordinary (B)
95:1-3,11-13	Christmas Midnight (A,B,C)
95:1,3-5,7-10	29th Ordinary (A)
	2nd Ordinary (C)
95:1-7	Dedication of the Lateran Basilica
96:1-2,6-7,9	7th Easter (C)
96:1-2,5-6,9	The Transfiguration
96:1-2,6-9	27th Ordinary (C)
96:1,6,11-12	Christmas Dawn (A,B,C)
97:1-6	Christmas Day (A,B,C)

97:1-4	6th Easter (B)
	28th Ordinary (C)
	The Immaculate Conception
97:5-9	33rd Ordinary (C)
99:1-3,5	11th Ordinary (A)
	4th Easter (C)
102:1-2,11-12,19-20	7th Easter (B)
102:1-4,8,10,12-13	7th Ordinary (A)
	8th Ordinary (B)
	7th Ordinary (C)
102:1-4,6-8,11	3rd Lent (C)
102:1-4,9-12	24th Ordinary (A)
103:1-4,24-25,27-30	Baptism of the Lord (C)
103:1,24,29-31,34	Pentecost (A,B,C)
104:1-6,8-9	Holy Family (B)
106:23-26,28-31	12th Ordinary (B)
109:1-4	The Body and Blood of Christ (C)
111:4-9	5th Ordinary (A)
112:1-2,4-8	25th Ordinary (C)
114:1-6,8-9	24th Ordinary (B)
115:10,15-19	2nd Lent (B)
115:12-13,15-18	The Body and Blood of Christ (B)
116:1-2 + Mark 16:15	9th Ordinary (C)
	21st Ordinary (C)
117:1-2,16-17,22-23	Easter Sunday (A,B,C)
117:2-4,13-15,22-24	2nd Easter (A)
117:2-4,15-18,22-24	2nd Easter (B)
117:2-4,22-27	2nd Easter (C)
117:1,8-9,21-23,26,28-29	4th Easter (B)
118:1-2,4-5,17-18,33-34	6th Ordinary (A)
118:57,72,76,77,127-130	17th Ordinary (A)
120	28th Ordinary (C)
121:1-2,4-9	1st Advent (A)
121:1-5	34th Ordinary (C)
122	14th Ordinary (B)

125	30th Ordinary (B)
	2nd Advent (C)
	5th Lent (C)
127:1-5	Holy Family (A)
	33rd Ordinary (A)
	27th Ordinary (B)
129	5th Lent (A)
	10th Ordinary (B)
130	31st Ordinary (A)
136:1-6	4th Lent (B)
137:1-5,7-8	5th Ordinary (C)
137:1-3,6,8	21st Ordinary (A)
137:1-3,6-8	17th Ordinary (C)
138:1-3,13-15	Birth of John the Baptist
144:1-2,8-11,13-14	14th Ordinary (A)
	31st Ordinary (C)
144:2-3,8-9,17-18	25th Ordinary (A)
144:8-9,15-18	18th Ordinary (A)
144:8-13	5th Easter (C)
144:10-11,15-18	17th Ordinary (B)
145:1,7-10	23rd Ordinary (B)
145:2,6-10	26th Ordinary (C)
145:2,7-10	32nd Ordinary (B)
145:6-10	3rd Advent (A)
145:7-10	4th Ordinary (A)
146:1-6	5th Ordinary (B)
147:12-15,19-20	2nd after Christmas (A,B,C)
	The Body and Blood of Christ (A)

Canticles

Isaiah 12:2-6	Baptism of the Lord (B)
	3rd Advent (C)
Daniel 3:32,52-56	Trinity (A)
Luke 1:46-50,53-54	3rd Advent (B)